EXTREME RAPID WEIGHT LOSS HYPNOSIS FOR WOMEN

*Stop Food Addiction and Eat Healthy with
Hypnotic Gastric Band.
Powerful Hypnosis Psychology, Guided
Meditations, Affirmation for Women Who
Want Fat Burn.
Extreme Diet, Emotional Eating, Manifestation,
Mini Habits, Deep Sleep, Past Life Regression.
Increase Your Motivation, Self Esteem, and
Confidence.
Overcome Anxiety, Stress, Depression, and Worry*

DR. LUIS CAMBELL & SEBI CAMPBELL

D1574473

Table of Contents

Introduction

Hypnosis weight loss is a natural, lasting, and profoundly impactful weight loss habit that you can use to change the way you approach weight loss, ultimately, and food in general, for the rest of your life.

With Hypnosis, you are not ingesting anything that results in Hypnosis working. Instead, you are merely listening to guided hypnosis meditations that help you transform the way your subconscious mind works. As you change the way your subconscious mind works, you will find yourself not even having cravings or unhealthy food urges in the first place.

This means no more fighting against your desires, yo-yo dieting, "falling off the wagon," or experiencing any inner conflict around your eating patterns or weight loss exercises that help you lose weight. Instead, you will begin to have an entirely new mindset and perspective around weight loss, leading to you having more success in losing weight and keeping it off for good.

In addition to Hypnosis itself being productive, you can also combine Hypnosis with any other weight loss strategy you are using. Changed dietary behaviors, exercise routines, any medications you may be taking with your medical practitioner's advisement, and any other weight loss practices you may be engaging in can all safely be done with Hypnosis. By including Hypnosis in your existing weight loss routines, you can improve your effectiveness and rapidly increase the success you experience in your weight loss patterns.

Finally, Hypnosis can be beneficial for many things beyond weight loss. One of the side effects that you will likely notice once you start using Hypnosis to help change your weight loss experience is that you also experience a boost in your confidence, self-esteem, and general feelings of positivity. Many people who use Hypnosis regularly find themselves feeling more positive and in better spirits in general. Still, you will also feel incredible and will have a happy and cheerful mood as well.

Chapter 1. How does the mind work?

The weight loss industry is common knowledge that merely a diet or a weight loss program does not ensure lasting weight loss results. You will invariably recover all weight if you do not assume that you are slim and strong for life in your unconscious mind. This is one area that is lacking in most weight reduction programs. There is, however, a way to complete this missing link.

We prefer to think of our minds and bodies as being entirely different entities, but in fact, the two of them are linked more closely than we would think.

If you have ever read of people getting minor surgery under the influence of nothing but hypnosis, you will know this is valid. Of course, most of us are glad to have an anesthetic under these conditions, but it shows just how strong the mind can be!

Can The Mind Affect The Body's Wellbeing?

Yes, it does - which is why it pays dividends to focus on using the mind's power in a meaningful way. We all can think either positive or negative thoughts every second of the day. If we want to think negatively, it can have a profound impact on our physical wellbeing.

For instance, you can be the type of person who gets depressed and nervous quite faster. If anything happens to make you feel like this, it can affect how your body responds to the situation; however. You can improve.

If you find yourself in a queue, for example, and usually start feeling stressed at the amount of time you are wasting, change your thinking. Take some deep breaths and think of good things.

You can also use the time constructively and efficiently, maybe by talking to the person next to you.

The argument is that you should be optimistic in this situation. You choose to run out of the store. After all, you had to wait or feel satisfied because you had a good talk with someone.

Take care of the bond between mind and body.

Try now to understand how your emotions affect the physical way you feel. Stress can influence us in many ways, and long-term stress does little good to anyone. If you know that you are prone to high pressure, try and alleviate it by using your mind's strength.

Start with the mind and follow the rest.

This is just as true when you start a new course or launch a new business with weight loss. The idea is that you must first persuade your unconscious mind that you want to lose weight and that you are a lean and balanced person. It would help if you fed these suggestions in your subconscious self so that your mind can guide you to the most feasible alternatives that will realize these suggestions.

Scientific evidence suggests that our capacity to receive feedback is dependent on a specific state of mind, a kind of modified form of reason. This state of mind is a departure from ordinary consciousness, which primarily functions under the Beta brainwave.

When it works, the brain produces electrochemical discharges. However, there are different feature levels. You are in beta while you work at your "alert" daytime stage -

talk to friends, speak to someone, read, solve a chemical equation, or write an essay.

Beta waves range in frequency from 15 to 40 cycles per second. This is the usual brainwave frequency during the day.

When you sit back after chemistry problems have been solved, you are in an Alpha state.

When you sit on the train, you are in the Alpha state, and you watch the scenery flowing while your thoughts go on their journey. It also places you in this state to pray or meditate.

Alpha brain waves are slower but bigger. Its frequency varies from 9-14 cycles per second. When you are comfortable in this state, you feel calm and safe. You have muscles and are open to suggestions. The few minutes you spend relaxing before falling asleep is Alpha state.

It's best to reprogram yourself to the Alpha state. Eighty-five percent of all medical issues (including overeating and weight problems) include unresolved body pain and stress. Getting to Alpha would help you unquestionably disrupt this unresolved stress and make your diet more incremental. Moreover, when you think about Alpha, you can easily reprogram yourself.

Begin by taking the time to relax.

A meditative, peaceful day is 20-30 minutes long enough. Build a deep breathing routine that focuses your mind on a sentence, sound, or mantra. The significance of the sound or word is not as critical as it evokes in you. When your body stress has loosened, feed your mind with positive images.

Visualize the optimal weight.

Focus on your slim, lean body and shapely legs. Imagine for yourself a solid and dynamic life. Make it a regular practice for your ideal self in this enabling visualization until you can truly see yourself as lean, strong, and beautiful. Next time you feel like wolfing a chocolate cake, turning your mind into a slim body and slim legs.

It was pretty hard for me to think I should go back to size 4 when I got extra weight during menopause. Now the hormonal shifts make it impossible for me to be what I was in my twenties." I recalled then that I used the same argument as I had made during my pregnancy: "Mothers should gain weight."

We seem to depend on generally accepted hypotheses to determine. Do you know that your body can be carved as you want? You're 99 percent water and quantum space, and when you see it, the body isn't thrown into stone or tissue.

Besides, the visual cortex at the back of the skull creates what you see in your brain from a network of chemical and electric charges, and your visual cortex pattern varies with the way that I or someone else creates. You don't see anything out there. If you notice, here you make things (your mind).

Now we are freed by that physiological fact - and we know that we can create what we want now, and we can do it anyway if it's not what we want!!!

What can we do?

1. Protein creates a lean body mass, giving the body youthful strength by eating low-fat protein (not too much animal protein combined with fat and calories).

2. We can begin a workout like tennis, skating, walking.

3. We should love healthy, nutritious food and eat good food.

4. We should stay away from those who are trying to destroy our morale.

We are responsible for who we are going to be. Nothing ties us to interest but our sense of constraint!

Meditation is a good beginning, but you can't do it in a queue, of course!

Some people are more optimistic than others, but fortunately, you will become more positive when trying to make things happen. A healthy way to start the link between mind and body is to exercise regularly.

First of all, a short walk in the morning wakes your mind up; it alarms you completely and helps your body feel-good hormones. It also has fantastic physical results and makes you feel more optimistic as the day progresses.

Training the Mind For Positive Output

Psychology gave us a range of resources in programming behavioral transformations and thought improvements to improve an individual's mental condition or to help this person better face daily truths.

Various approaches, such as meditation, hypnosis, and sleep programming, maybe studied clinically. However, mind exercises and tests with mental stimuli enable those who want to train their minds and provide subtle training to improve the mind's power.

The mind has already been pre-programmed from our previous experiences and learning.

Our memory fuels continue to work and provide the basis for reference and contrast to items that are currently found.

Any effort to modify what is already in mind, to adapt previously conceived notions, and to ensure that the reason can tolerate more than it has done in the past requires a compelling change of attitude in a person. After all, every person determines how they interpret what they see and perceive and what they imagine.

It is still our intellect that gathers all the knowledge our brain has gone through. However powerful the brain is, one should note that it is still only a human tool, and at the end of the day, it is our complete selves that will continue to develop and progress.

It is not easy to program mind perceptions, particularly for cynics and realists. Instead of a fluid flow of brain functions, negative thoughts block excellent ideas stored in our memory banks, giving our minds a stricter time to filter out which environmental elements are assets to achieve our idyllic state. It is also essential to maintain a positive attitude as this will help us decide what we want and which things move.

This optimistic way of thinking is helped more easily by adding each experience equal to our excellence or ideal norm. If we have a specific situation and can achieve it with our brains' power, we will have a greater probability of achieving the same success in the future.

This is all due to the adapted way of thinking we now have because of the previous performance. Constructive thought can indeed do a lot because it clears the mind and makes it easier to think about the ideal.

We must be in complete control in programming mind sequences, ideas, and memories for performance. We have to know what we want and how we want it to be done, and we must learn to think, dream and envision it ourselves and our minds, and we'll know soon that we live it already.

Hypnosis Mind Control

The mental stimulation of hypnosis, for many, is quite a fascinating topic. For decades, theories have circulated about how others might exploit an unsuspecting person's mind to bid.

These claims may include some details because hypnosis is a scientific method for helping people overcome something.

This is why, today, many people want to learn more about the mental stimulation of hypnosis.

In hypnosis, a person is in a high focus while his body is relaxed. A hypnotist can make suggestions at this point to change something in the individual. It can be his attitude or his way of thinking or his way of seeing others. These suggestions may, according to the hypnotist, be an advantage or a disadvantage.

In reality, hypnosis mind control essentially creates a connection between the subconscious and the person's mind and body to change his mind without instruments. Studies have shown that the mental power of hypnosis will change behavior whenever it is used. There are many ways in which hypnosis behavioral control methods are now used.

It can help those who have trouble overcoming their addiction. In some cases, hypnosis mental control is often used to develop relationships with other people, which marketing people need.

Hypnosis mental control is a technique that, if implemented correctly, can create positive changes in an individual. People are watchful when placed under hypnosis, but their minds are relaxed so that ideas can easily reach the mind.

Those who have undergone these strategies reflect on how their perspective has changed and how their fears and addiction are healed in some instances. In addition to its benefit, hypnosis may also have such defects.

Some people use these methods to manipulate others in scams or theft, particularly on the disadvantages of using this strategy. Many familiar with hypnosis methods can faster apply them to criminals to make decisions about them. Hypnosis should not be feared because it does not do irreversible damage or harm to the way a person thinks.

It is best to bear in mind that hypnosis or mind control is a mechanism where the subconscious mind is suggested with no damage. Different hypnosis methods are available that people may apply to themselves or others.

However, having a hypnotherapist is advised for those with severe issues because they can faster deepen their minds. This means that any problems they have will hopefully be cured in no time.

Mind control has achieved a high degree of popularity, which is why there are many websites today that offer hypnosis courses. It is certainly possible to learn how to use hypnosis. All that is needed is a desire to learn and an open mind.

Those that are more open-minded about hypnosis are more likely to practice the art of hypnosis over others. Only sit back and enjoy studying mind control strategies in your own house.

Everyday Mental Struggles That Manifest Themselves In The Body

Now that you understand how a person's internal environment can lead them to fall into a cycle of emotional eating or seek food as comfort and eventually become overweight, we will look at some of the factors that lead people to develop a tumultuous internal environment.

Several types of emotional deficiencies or causes can lead a person to develop disordered eating, resulting in weight gain over time. We will explore some of these factors in detail in hopes that you will recognize some of the reasons why you may experience struggles with eating or with weight loss.

Childhood Trauma

The first example of an emotional deficiency that we will examine is more of an umbrella for various emotional deficits. This umbrella term is Childhood Causes. If you think back on your childhood, think about how your relationship with food was cultivated. Maybe you were taught that when you behaved, you received food as a reward. Maybe when you were feeling down, you were given food to cheer you up. Maybe you turned to food when you were experiencing negative events that happened during your childhood.

Another cause could be the relationship you had with your parents or the relationship to food modeled for you in your formative years.

Maybe you grew up in an emotionally abusive home, and food was the only comfort you had. These reasons are completely valid, which was the only way you knew how to deal with problems when you were a child. The positive thing is that you can take control of your life and make lasting changes for the better now that you are an adult.

Any of these experiences could cause someone to suffer from emotional eating in their adulthood, as it had become something learned from an early age. This type of emotional deficiency is quite challenging to break as it has likely been a habit for many, many years, but it is possible. When we are children, we learn habits and make associations without knowing it that we often carry into our later lives. While this is no fault of yours, recognizing it as a potential issue is essential to make changes.

Covering Up Your Emotions

Another emotional deficiency that can manifest itself in emotional eating and food cravings is the effort to cover up our emotions. Sometimes we would instead distract ourselves and cover up our feelings than to feel them or to face them head-on. In this case, our brain may make us feel hungry to delight us with the act of eating food. When we have a quiet minute where these feelings or thoughts pop into our minds, we can cover them up by deciding to prepare food and eat and convince ourselves that we are "too busy" to acknowledge our feelings because we have to deal with our hunger. The fact that it is a hunger that arises in this scenario makes it very difficult to ignore and very easy to deem as a necessary distraction. After all, we do need to eat to survive. This necessity can be a problem, though, if we do not require nourishment and we are telling ourselves that this is why we cannot deal with our demons or our emotions.

If there is something that you think you may be avoiding dealing with or thinking about, or if you tend to be very uncomfortable with feelings of unrest, you may be experiencing this type of emotional eating.

Feeling Empty Or Feeling Bored

When we feel bored, we often decide to eat or decide that we are hungry. This hunger occupies our mind and our time and makes us feel less bored and even feel positive and happy. We also may eat when we are feeling empty. When we feel empty, the food will quite literally be ingested to fill a void. Still, as we know, the food will not fill an emotional gap in sort, which will lead to an unhealthy cycle of trying to fill ourselves emotionally with something that will never actually work. This process will lead us to become disappointed every time and continue trying to fill this void with material things like food or purchases. This compulsion can also be caused because of a general feeling of dissatisfaction with life and lack of something in your life. Looking deeper into this the next time you feel those cravings will be difficult but will help you greatly in the long term as you will then be able to identify the source of your feelings of emptiness and begin to fill these voids in ways that will be much more effective.

Experiencing An Affection Deficiency

Another emotional deficiency that could manifest itself as food cravings is an affection deficiency. This type of deficiency can be feelings of loneliness, emotions of a lack of love, or undesired feelings. Suppose a person has been without an intimate relationship or has recently gone through a breakup, or has not experienced physical intimacy in quite some time. In that case, they may be experiencing an affection deficiency.

This type of emotional deficiency will often manifest itself in food cravings.

Low Self-Esteem

Another emotional deficiency that food cravings may indicate is a low level of self-esteem. Low self-esteem can cause people to feel down, unlovable, inadequate, and overall negative and sad. This feeling can make a person feel like eating foods they enjoy will make them feel better, even for a mere few moments. Low self-esteem is an emotional deficiency that is difficult to deal with, as it affects every area of a person's life, such as their love life, social life, career life, etc. Sometimes, people have reported feeling like food was always there for them and never left them. While this is true, they will often be left feeling even emptier and lower about themselves after giving into cravings.

Low Mood

A general low mood can cause emotional eating. While the problem of emotional eating is something that is occurring multiple times per week, and we all have general low moods or bad days, if this makes you crave food and especially food of an unhealthy sort, this could become emotional eating. When we feel down or are having a bad day, we want to eat food to make ourselves feel better; this is emotional eating. Some people will enjoy a drink at the end of a bad day. If this happens every once in a while, it is not necessarily a problem with emotional eating. The more often it happens, the more often it is emotional eating. Further, we do not have to give in to the cravings to be considered emotional eating.

Experiencing the cravings often and in tandem with negative feelings in the first place is what constitutes emotional eating.

Depression

Suffering from depression also can lead to emotional eating. Depression is a constant low mood for months on end, and this low mood can cause a person to turn to food for comfort and a lift in spirit. This lifting feeling can then become emotional eating in addition to and because of depression.

Anxiety

Having anxiety can lead to emotional eating, as well. There are several types of stress, and whether it is general anxiety (constant levels of pressure), situational anxiety (triggered by a situation or scenario), can lead to emotional eating. You have likely heard of the term *comfort food* to describe certain foods and dishes. The reason for this is because they are usually foods rich in carbohydrates, fats, and heavy. These foods bring people a sense of comfort. These foods are often turned to when people suffering from anxiety are emotionally eating because they temporarily ease their stress and make them feel calmer and more at ease. This calming effect only lasts for a short period; however, before their anxiety usually gears up again.

Stress

Stress eating is probably the most common form of emotional eating. While this does not become an issue for everyone experiencing stress, it is a problem for people who consistently turn to food to ease their anxiety.

Some people are always under pressure, and they will constantly be looking for ways to alleviate their stress.

Food is one of these ways that people use to make themselves feel better and to take their minds off of their stress. As with all of the other examples we have seen above, this is not a lasting resolution, and it becomes a cycle.

The Media

The constant exposure to media that we experience daily can lead to a hostile internal environment over time. If you are constantly seeing photos of people who make you feel inadequate, or people to whom you are comparing yourself, you can begin to believe that you are not good enough or that you will never measure up. These thoughts can be damaging and can lead a person to turn to food for comfort. This coping mechanism can lead them to feel worse about themselves afterward, leading to even more emotional eating.

Chapter 2. Hypnotherapy and Hypnosis

Hypnosis and hypnotherapy are often described as being one in the same practice, but they are not. Hypnotherapy is a technique used by hypnotists to treat a subject's concern or problem. In this kind of situation, the subconscious mind is more accessible where habits, memory, and emotions are located, which allows the hypnotist to aid and guide a subject to achieve long-lasting and positive changes in their lives.

Hypnotherapy is a kind of guided hypnosis that mainly focuses on concentration, while hypnosis refers to the act of guiding an individual into a trance state of mind. With hypnosis, this state is commonly referred to as either a resting state of relaxation, induced suggestibility, or hyper-focus.

The average student or individual working battles with every day is to keep focus during their daily routine. A consistent lack of focus may leave a person feeling tired, unmotivated, stressed, and inefficient. That's just one of the main reasons why hypnotherapy serves as the ultimate solution for anyone looking to improve productivity, relieve stress and anxiety, and boost their overall health.

Hypnotherapy is used in various instances, all of which have been proven to be very effective. It is similar to other types of psychological treatments with benefits that are similar to those of psychotherapy.

The practice treats conditions, including phobias, anxiety disorders, bad habits, weight gain, substance abuse, learning disorders, poor communication skills, and even pain. It can resolve digestive and gastrointestinal disorders and severe hormonal skin disorders, aiding as a massive solution to many different issues people face daily and are often unaware of how to treat.

Many patients with immune disorders or severe conditions, such as cancer, can also be treated with hypnotherapy as it is known for its pain-relieving abilities. It is beneficial and used when patients undergo chemotherapy or physical rehabilitation that is excessively painful.

A therapist carries out hypnotherapy in a therapeutic and tranquil environment that allows the patient to enter and remain in a focused state of mind. Apart from its incredible benefits, it can adjust the reason and shift mental behavior, almost tricking the brain into focusing on positive intentions. Often, with severe cases, such as advanced stages of cancer, patients are almost convinced that they will not live very long. Some may even receive their expected date of passing from their medical practitioner.

Faced with extreme negativity, such as a patient being told that they will die, patients tend to give up.

Now, regardless of what you believe, what your mind conceives to believe may very well become a reality. This thinking manner holds a lot of truth and could set a patient apart from surviving their condition. Although it is difficult to achieve a state of mind where one is cheerful when faced with illness, hypnotherapy can adjust one's thought process and retrain the brain into thinking only positive thoughts.

In essence, a cancer patient's attitude can massively contribute to their probability of healing. Hypnotherapy can relieve pain and add a mental shield against negative thinking processes that could contribute to a patient's inability to recover.

From various recovery types, acting as more than just a supportive release for pain, emotional and mental stability, something many individuals find fascinating is that one can lose weight with hypnotherapy.

Depending on how severe the problem being treated is, hypnotherapy may take longer to see a difference. Upon meeting with a hypnotherapist, the practitioner will assess the extent of hypnotherapy required, measured in hours, for the patient to obtain the result they would like to see at the end of their therapy course. A specific total number of hours will be prescribed to the patient, forming a part of alternative healthcare.

Take it as a tip, with hypnotherapy, and it is essential to feel comfortable with your practitioner, which is why you must seek out several to find the right one. With hypnotherapy, it's always a good idea to ask around for recommendations and not settle for the first therapist you come across.

Since you now have a good understanding of hypnotherapy, it's also necessary to be informed about hypnosis.

Hypnosis refers to placing an individual in a trance state of mind, referred to as deep relaxation, increased suggestibility, and hyper-focus.

Thinking about the different references related to hypnosis, one may think of it as being focused on deep sleep. When we sleep, we tend to enter and exit a trance state quite often. This can also occur when we listen to music or focus on reading a book or watching a movie. It invites a state of mind where our thought processes almost come to a halt as we are focused, and our brain suddenly even more so than it is used to. Whenever you immerse yourself in something and focus, you enter a trance state of mind.

So, what's the difference between professional hypnosis, the actual act of induced hypnosis, and our brief everyday moments of intense focus?

The only difference is that with hypnosis, you are assisted by a hypnotherapist to enter a trance state of mind where you can achieve beautiful things. You can earn a form of motivation, positivity, healing, stress-relief, and even weight loss.

The Myths:

Those who believe in myths or are superstitious have painted a picture of hypnosis that has managed to scare people away.

Whether you've heard about hypnosis in the media, saw it in a movie, or were shunned by your parents for learning more about it, you can rest assured that it's not as bad as society makes it out to be.

Can hypnotists control the minds of their patients? Of course not. Hypnosis is used as a medical practice to relieve symptoms associated with pain, anxiety or help people lose weight and get back on the healthy train again. It doesn't leave you feeling helpless or unaware of what you're doing.

During hypnotherapy, patients are still conscious and can hear everything around them, which is another reason it is considered an entirely safe practice. To assure people even more, it is next to impossible for anyone to be unconscious when undergoing hypnosis.

Differentiating between hypnosis and hypnotherapy, you now have learned that both practices have a similar foundation and help patients achieve different goals. Both methods can indeed help patients lose weight.

When you want to lose weight, you have to focus on different things. Losing weight is never just about cleaning up your diet and incorporating exercise into your daily routine.

Since stress is a significant part of why our bodies hold onto weight, hypnosis serves as the perfect solution to relieve stress and manage disorders, often contributing to weight gain. This includes both anxiety and depression. Additionally, it can help individuals with either an overactive or underactive thyroid reach some balance level, allowing one's body to lose weight permanently and sustainably.

On the other hand, hypnotherapy is perfect for treating many different cases, including bad habits like smoking and overeating, which can contribute to a variety of eating disorders. Both can help you develop a bad relationship with food and even act to cope with stress. That is why hypnosis and hypnotherapy can work hand-in-hand to achieve possible results, depending on your needs. Hypnotherapy also relieves mind-body illnesses and reduces symptoms, including irritable bowel syndrome, skin conditions, and various addictions.

Unless you suffer from severe stress-related disorders that require you to engage in both practices, hypnotherapy can serve all of your needs concerning weight loss. It is the perfect option for anyone aiming to achieve long-term results.

Given that every decision, thought, and intention is birthed in mind, it's pretty simple to see why hypnotherapy can solve many of the problems we as humans face with our bodies today.

Both hypnosis and hypnotherapy serve as practices that help deplete negative habits and assist anyone, no matter how sick or unmotivated, to get back on track, follow a healthy diet, and attainable exercise program as kick many harmful addictions.

Chapter 3. Different Techniques of Hypnosis

Count Your Breath

For people who are not particularly attracted to the physical, verbal, or visual practices to help them enter a hypnotic state, there are many types of mindfulness practices that you can engage in to begin your self-hypnosis. Many of these involve you using your breath to enter a hypnotic state. You can do this by using the following steps for counting your breath to enter your deep trance.

The idea of this practice is to be able to count as many breaths as you can before you lose focus on your breathing. Know that if you are brand new to meditation and hypnosis that you likely will not be able to count very high in the beginning. Instead, you may only count to a count of 2 or 3. This is completely fine and can still be valuable, so do not refrain from using this practice just because you don't make it to a particularly high number.

When you are ready, you want to get yourself into a comfortable position. With self-hypnosis, you should either be sitting or lying down. Then, go ahead and close your eyes and get relaxed. If you cannot keep your eyes closed, it is perfectly okay to keep them open. Simply keep them relaxed and focus on one area in front of you that does not steal your attention or focus easily, such as a blank spot on the wall or ceiling.

Now, begin breathing at a relaxed and comfortable pace. Do not try and control your breath. Rather, relax and pay attention to it as it comes naturally. Then, as it comes, begin counting your breath. Count as many as you can without rushing them, or otherwise influencing them to change.

If you notice your awareness is being drawn away or that you are not able to stay focused, you can simply allow your thoughts to come and then let them leave on their own, too. Then, draw your awareness back to your breath.

You want to practice this as many times as you comfortably can. If you find that it is getting harder and harder to focus, that you are beginning to feel frustrated, or that you are otherwise working against hypnosis, then you can stop. As you continue to practice this, you will find that you can count your breath longer and that you stay in your hypnotic state longer, too.

This practice is very similar to what you are taught to practice in meditation, as it essentially is a form of meditation. Like meditation, entering a hypnotic state requires you to get into a deep state of relaxation. Therefore, using the same techniques you do to meditate can be a great way to enter your hypnotic state and begin practicing self-hypnosis.

Detailed Breathing

Detailed breathing is a form of breathing whereby you pass through any need to count and instead you will focus on details or sensations within your body. While you can typically do this in any way that you prefer, there is also a pattern you can follow to help you stay focused and present with your breathing practice. It is as follows.

Begin by finding a comfortable place to sit or lie down so that you can begin your self-hypnosis. You can choose anywhere that is going to allow you to stay focused without interruption for as long as possible.

When you are ready, draw your awareness to your breath. Do not attempt to control it in any way, rather notice how it is in its natural state.

Then, take a nice relaxing, deep breath in. As you do, notice any sensations you may feel on, in, or around your nose. Notice these sensations as you breathe out, too. When you are ready, do it again. Then, again. You want to complete this detailed breathing practice through three breaths, with all of your body parts. You can follow this list if you need to recall what parts you should focus on:

- Your cheeks

- Your eyes and forehead

- Your scalp

- Your neck

- Your shoulder blades

- Your middle back

- Your lower back

- Your hips

- Your glutes

- The backs of your thighs

- Behind your knees

- Your calves

- The heels of your feet

- The balls of your feet

- Your toes

- The tops of your feet

- Your ankle

- Your shins

- Your knees

- The front of your thighs

- Your pelvis

- Your lower abdomen

- Your solar plexus

- Your rib cage

- Your chest

- Your throat

- Your chin

- Your mouth

- Your nose

Once you have completed your entire body, you should be in a completely relaxed state so that you can begin directing your self-hypnosis on whatever your intention is.

In the beginning, you may find it difficult to complete this entire detailed breathing practice. Instead, you may wish to focus on larger areas such as your face, head, torso, arms, hands, legs, and feet. Then, you can become more detailed the more you practice.

Pyramid Breathing

Pyramid breathing is another breathing practice you can use to enter your hypnotic state and begin self-hypnosis. This practice includes something that is known as mindful movement, which is an intentional movement that you will practice within your body to locate physical stress or resistance and bring your awareness to gently releasing this feeling. For example, pressing against a wall, curling your toes, stretching your shoulders, or otherwise physically moving your body and noticing any resistance you may feel. The idea is that you want to actually experience the resistance and then let it gradually eliminate itself through mindful intention. You can complete this practice using the following steps.

Begin by taking a deep breath and focusing on your breath. You do not need to count as high as you can, rather, but simply relax into three or four counted breaths.

When you are ready, gently move part of your body. This is a mindful movement you can practice. You may choose which movement you want to make based on where you can physically feel resistance in your body. For example, if you feel physical resistance in your chest, you can gently raise your arms above your head and feel that resistance and the many ways that it is physically affecting you.

Notice all of the pressures in your body and any sensations you may experience as a result of these movements.

When you are ready, go ahead and take another breath and then perform another mindful movement. Once again, take your time to notice any physical resistances, pains, or other sensations you may notice in this area of your body. Feel into them, and try and take the time to become aware of why they are there and what you may be able to do to consciously and subconsciously release them completely.

You want to continue practicing this over and over again through any resistance you may have. You may even repeat this practice with persistent sensations if you want to so that you can completely release them and let them go.

Doing this all the way through is a great way to allow you to enter a calmer state of mind. Once you have acknowledged all of these physical sensations and how they are affecting your body, you will likely notice how much more relaxed your mind is. Then, you can go ahead and begin directing your self-hypnosis practice.

Visual Exploration

For some people, creating a static visualization can be difficult and can result in them not being able to visualize anything. In this case, it may be beneficial to engage in visual exploration. This is essentially a form of visualization whereby you visualize a place that you are familiar with and add an explorative measure to it. For example, exploring the home in which you live. To do so, use the following steps to get started.

Start by sitting somewhere relaxing and closing your eyes. The entire visualization will be done with your eyes closed, to ensure that you are comfortable enough that you can stay still and keep your eyes closed for this entire practice.

Start by creating a basic visual of a room that you are familiar with within your mind, now. Then, begin exploring this room. As you are adding the details, visualize yourself walking around and touching them or interacting with them. For example, sit on a couch, run your hand over the wall, or pick up an object and begin exploring it with your hands.

After you have completely designed the first room in your mind and have interacted with various elements of the room, you want to begin exploring other elements. Go ahead and leave that room and build the next room. Whether it's a hallway, another room, or even outside, go ahead and begin following the same practices. Enter the room and begin exploring that one. As you are decorating it in your mind, interact with the decorations that are there.

Continue doing this with several rooms until you notice that you are in a hypnotic state and that you are ready to begin using the driven intention behind your self-hypnosis to achieve your results.

A Mental Pantomimed

This is a visual-meets-physical practice that can help those who are aided by visuals but who also like to be in motion. You can use this to begin visually seeing things in your mind but also cementing them in using physical movements.

For this practice, you are again going to begin visualizing a room that you are familiar with. You want to pick one where you will know as many details about the room as possible. Then, you will mentally describe them to yourself as you pantomime the actions associated with that room. For example, if you are explaining that the room is large, you might spread your arms wide to physically symbolize the largeness of the room. If you are talking about the window in the room, you might consider opening the window and then physically act out the process of opening the window.

For some people, incorporating as many sensations into their visualization as possible can strengthen your visualization practice. Eventually, you should be able to eliminate the pantomiming and verbal descriptions so that you can begin visualizing even deeper and more effectively, thus strengthening your ability to enter a self-hypnotic state.

Chapter 4. Hypnosis session to improve the relationship with food

When it comes to tricky connections, the guidance can often make a stride back or break; however, with food, that is not generally an alternative. We, as a whole, need to eat. However, for those of us who have a violent relationship with food, essential assignments like food shopping, eating out, or in any event, choosing what to cook at home can feel like a minefield.

As indicated by the insights, we've seen a 24% expansion in stoutness-related medical clinic affirmations in the UK over the late years. Over a third (35%) of grown-ups in England are overweight, with a further 28% being assessed to fall into the fat classification. However, notwithstanding a perpetual stream of government-maneuvered plans to get us into week-by-week weight loss classes, diets simply don't work for vast numbers of us. Yet, why would that be, and is there a more feasible approach to improve our relationship with what we eat?

For What Reason Diets Don't Work?

Confining what we eat, following unbending diet plans, or going to week-by-week gatherings accomplish specific individuals' work. Nonetheless, this can often be a temporary arrangement that drives numerous to encounter yo-yo dieting, weight loss, and weight gain. Trance specialist Becca Teers clarifies more. Many diet plans are impermanent and can be difficult to keep up on a progressing premise, often because they are excessively prohibitive or they absolutely deny us of our preferred nourishments."

So while we may see transient victories, because we aren't testing our general view of food, just as any hidden issues that may have led to undesirable eating practices, (for example, utilizing food as a method for dealing with stress), we aren't setting ourselves up for long haul achievement.

Indeed, Becca clarifies, we could be making a more negative cycle for ourselves. "By making us tally calories or deliberately measure elixir size or even exclude kinds of nourishments, numerous diets can make us more fixated on food and our eating. This can remove the delight from eating, and can lead us to pine for a greater amount of specific nourishments. A diet, gorge/gorge cycle can begin."

By making our center around the possibility that what we eat—and any related weight stresses—are simply the consequence of resolve, and are something we simply need to 'invest more energy' to change, diets can lead us to disregard the basic issues that are truly making us battle.

Risky associations with food aren't 'simply down to 'self-discipline.' Chaotic timetables, perspectives to food while growing up, and oblivious feelings, convictions, or practices that we might be uninformed we have created would all be able to prompt undesirable associations with food. Regardless of whether you battle with settling on more beneficial food decisions, indulging, or object to 'particular eating,' the odds are that there is a hidden issue that you may not know about—or that you may not realize how to fix. A portion of the typical reasons individuals can build up an undesirable relationship with food can include:

- *Solace Eating.* Otherwise called enthusiastic eating, a few people go to food as a method of adapting to testing contemplations, sentiments, feelings, or circumstances. If you wind up going after a bite when you are vexed or focused on, use food as an approach to rouse yourself to traverse an intense assignment or defeat fatigue. These are altogether signs that you may be utilizing food as an approach to support your temperament.

- *Stress.* Recognizing the indications of stress can be intense. When we feel overpowered and incapable of adapting, it tends to be a good sign that we're feeling the squeeze. In any case, for a few of us, our feelings of anxiety can steadily increment after some time, and we may not understand they are getting unmanageable as we attempt to discover approaches to self-cure to change how we are feeling.

We may see if our drinking increments as our feelings of anxiety do—going from a glass of wine to get over an upsetting day, up to three, four, or even an entire jug—yet shouldn't something be said about what we eat? This isn't to imply that every last extravagance is an indication of a more extensive issue, yet by its very nature, food—something we have to live, that we as a whole appreciate consistently—can turn out to be difficult to characterize concerning designs.

- *Food Addictions*. While there are still discussions encompassing the term 'food habit,' many can concur that what and how we eat, can fall under a sort of social compulsion. Certain nourishments that may cause spikes in feel-great synthetic substances or our vitality levels can lead us to briefly feeling extraordinary—yet often don't give us a continuous sentiment of being full or fulfilled. After some time, this can imply that we have to eat increasingly more of something to get that equivalent inclination. This can prompt further issues of sentiments of blame, disgrace, and can even contrarily affect your confidence and fearlessness.

- *Previous Existence Encounters*. Other essential variables from our pasts can affect our continuous perspectives and practices around food. Past injury, misuse, taken in courses from our families, difficulty adapting to negative feelings, pain, loss, or low confidence would all contribute.

- *It Became a Propensity*. After some time, negative behavior patterns can create without our understanding. Maybe you end up eating when you aren't ravenous, you generally purchase a nibble with your morning espresso, or you can't envision going out to the film without getting some popcorn. Identifying these propensities all alone can be dubious.

- *Wellbeing (Physical or Mental) Related Conditions.* Hormonal irregular characteristics, prescription results, and even certain psychological well-being conditions, such as melancholy or nervousness, would all be able to prompt unfortunate eating practices or issues with food. If you are concerned that another fundamental condition might be causing you eating issues, it's critical to talk with your GP.

By What Method Would Hypnotherapy Be Able to Help?

Working with a subliminal specialist can assist you with tending to a wide scope of issues and difficulties. A qualified, experienced advisor will have the option to assist you with identifying and address any fundamental reasons why you might be battling with food.

Hypnotherapy can help you figure out how to handle negative feelings in a better, sound, maintainable way that can permit you to keep away from comfort eating. For the individuals who eat or nibble without speculation, for example, when you're preparing or in the middle of dinners, if careful eating doesn't work for you, gastric band hypnotherapy might have the option to assist you with feeling full for more. This can help you with abstaining from touching on undesirable nourishments.

Through working with an accomplished trance inducer, you can learn new apparatuses and procedures to assist you with overseeing continuous or fluctuating feelings of anxiety, uneasiness, or passionate over-burden.

With their assistance and direction, you can all the more likely see how these might be influencing different aspects of your life, all in all, helping you to roll out sure improvements that can have a more extensive, continuous effect.

As Julia shares through her understanding of attempting hypnotherapy for enthusiastic eating, hypnosis can help you figure out how to speak with and comprehend your body more readily.

"It had arrived at where I'd become fixated [with food] and it wasn't extraordinary for me. I've gotten much less worried about eating. I appreciate it; however, I've figured out how to eat when my body is ravenous and not because my psyche needs something to relieve my feelings. Hypnotherapy has truly helped me to understand things."

"I have begun to become familiar with our interior examples, where they originate from, and how we approach evolving them."

Hypnotherapy Accomplishes Work?

A typical inquiry when it comes to hypnosis is: will it work for me? It's difficult to know until you attempt it yourself. Studies have indicated hypnotherapy can be a powerful alternative for facilitating uneasiness, treating certain addictions, and in any event, handling indulging.

Similarly, as with all types of hypnotherapy, it requires a receptive outlook, a craving for change, and commitment. A few people may see changes in conduct after only one meeting, while others may require a few to see genuine upgrades. Your trance specialist may present self-hypnosis strategies; you can attempt yourself between meetings to help strengthen novel thoughts and support progress.

Food is integral to life. What we devour can furnish us with vitality influences our temperament, just as how we see our bodies. We are generally extraordinary—as are our diets and lifestyles. To be sound all around, a stable relationship with food is significant.

Especially toward the beginning of the year, numerous individuals set themselves targets identified with food and their diets. Similarly, as with any objectives, those identified with food are close to home and will differ from individual to individual. However, regardless of whether you will likely get thinner, quit going after the sugar, or to expend more veggies, there are things that we all can do to improve our relationship with food as a rule:

Quit rebuffing yourself for what you ate yesterday

At some point or few days of eating off-plan or horribly won't fix your difficult work, or significantly hurt your objectives. If you had an awful day yesterday, make an effort not to overcompensate today—being excessively hard on yourself isn't the appropriate response. Make sure to appreciate life just like the food you eat.

You don't need to seek the ideal diet

Nobody is holding you to eating the 'flawless food' constantly. Indeed, even nourishment experts will have the most loved suppers that are less nutritious than others are. It's about parity.

Similarly, don't exclusively depend on food to make the scales shift. Recollect that food alone isn't sufficient to make changes for life that will last. Exercise, anyway much or little, is the thing that will make a solid lifestyle stick.

Try not to hold up until you're eager to eat

When we feel hungry, it can often be difficult to use sound judgment about food. You may need something that can be arranged rapidly or even eaten rapidly if you're in a surge. However, this isn't useful for long haul objectives.

Attempt to set up your food consistently—or possibly when you're not at home. Likewise, attempt to adhere to regular eating times and forestall hunger for the day's duration.

Quit utilizing food as a prize

Especially if you're attempting to get in shape. There are many thoughts to remunerate yourself in different manners, which can assist you with remaining on target and keeping you from building an enthusiastic association among remunerations and food.

Survey your passionate association with food

It is safe to say that you are as yet going after the tidbits, in any event, when you're not eager? This recommends there's something more profound going on. A hypnotherapy expert might have the option to assist you with arriving at the center of the issue. Why not look for help this year, and change your relationship with nourishment for good?

Food and our relationship to it shape how we carry on with our day-by-day lives. Now and again, it's simple, and we anticipate dinners, can adjust our diet, and use food to help a decent lifestyle. Occasionally, we separate, structure propensities around food that could be solid, and go to food to treat more profound hidden issues. This distinction is a brain-body disengagement and an absence of care. The seriousness of the last can be what leads or has led to dietary problems.

When you or a friend or family member are battling with dietary issues, and you're considering how to change your relationship with food, perused on here to see more about yourself and your dietary patterns. Make sure to contact your essential consideration supplier and a fundamental analyst if you feel that you or your adored one is in danger.

Our Entanglements with Food

For some, food is utilized far beyond simply refueling. You might be moving toward it for comfort, festivity, commitment, or different reasons. Indeed, even your state of mind can influence what and when you eat. Truth be told, contingent upon the day, the amount you eat changes. You could be gorging, under-eating, or just eating hastily because of all these outside elements. Instructions to change your relationship with food begins with understanding your food triggers.

Watch Your Hunger and When You Feel Hungry

Notice when you feel hungry. Regardless of whether you're eating because the clock says as much or you're stifling your craving because you're excessively occupied, it's an ideal opportunity to be more aware of what your body is letting you know. Remove your everyday circumstances from the condition and focus on when you're feeling hunger. Consider beginning a diary to note your mind-set's changes and how that may identify with when you want to eat when it is anything but suppertime.

Propensities around Cravings and Comfort Food

For the majority of us, cheap food and garbage have made their tricky ways into our diet, guaranteeing we desire them frequently. It's classified as "comfort food" on purpose! While trying to keep away from these, numerous individuals go to dieting. While diets will mention to you what to eat, they're often prohibitive, and it's anything, but difficult to fall into a pattern of eating excessively or excessively little

All in all, how would we change your relationship with food? It's an ideal opportunity to venture out of this example and reconnect with your body.

When you discharge yourself from judgment and blame, you get an opportunity to taste the food you're eating. Also, keeping in mind that frozen yogurt truly tastes great, you may understand that you appreciate feeding decisions like organic products, vegetables, and even quinoa.

Food as Reward and Punishment

It is anything but unexpected that numerous grown-ups use food as the carrot or the stick in their everyday lives. For some time, food has been a notable prize framework or a disciplined framework, either as desserts for supper or censure for not eating all your food as a component of the "perfect plate club." Is it conceivable to change such a profound, situated affiliation? We suspect as much. If you genuinely need to figure out how to change your relationship with food, this is essential.

Chapter 5. Why Your Body Gains Weight?

People become emotionally attached to food from infancy through adulthood. Children sometimes get rewarded with snacks or treats for healthy behavior; adults are often treated to dinner. There are numerous celebrations across the year from Christmas, Halloween, Thanksgiving, birthdays, and Valentine's Day. of these celebrations are food-focused. As people eat together, they feel good and happy.

It has also been proven that an aroma of a special quite baked cake can create an emotional connection memory that will last throughout someone's lifetime. Some foods are for nourishment, but others we take only for comfort, counting on how they create us feel. Whenever the brain reacts and feels pleasure for a specific food within our reach, most of the time, we'll grab it and eat it. During this point, the brain releases a chemical called dopamine, the method feels perfect, and if we equate the sensation with food, then the result is going to be negative.

High body mass index (BMI) is often linked to emotional problems like anxiety, depression, and stress. Those emotional issues can make one overindulge after a rough day at the office as a gift for an honest feeling. Some people use junk as a coping mechanism once they hear bad news. This habit is often only be improved by the utilization of meditation exercises to affect one's emotions, stress, or anxiety. Because the practices continue, and you pay close attention to your breath and allocate longer for thinking.

Types of Eating

We eat to survive, and without food, we'll die. Our body needs nutrients to function effectively. Eating because one is hungry is different from eating because there's food or one that desires to eat.

We need to coach our system in such how that we eat to curb hunger just a similar way we drink water to quench thirst. While food lovers explore different sorts of food, most of them are keen enough to include healthy eating in their diet.

Mindful Eating

This way is a framework wont to bring back one's relationship with food and eating experiences. During this technique, your presence is significant, and every one of the senses is engaged. As an example, how the food smells, the taste of the food, how appetizing it's, and lastly, your body's reaction to the feed.

By this, I mean how that specific food made you are feeling. Mindful eating always incorporates intuitive eating. It makes the body relax and hamper a touch bit as we hear the inner cues of real hunger.

Thus, helping us rectify and reduce emotional binge or emotional eating. Mindful eating can cause weight loss as long together makes the proper food choices. It's a way of eating that's psychologically controlled, and therefore the food portion measured counting on need. In mind eating, it doesn't matter what proportion of food is there.

What matters is that the quantity needed at that specific time. Eating thus becomes a response to hunger aside from a leisure activity. Rarely, People that follow this eating method suffer from obesity.

They're physically fit and healthy. During eating also there's no rush, no matter whether one is late or not. The chewing is simultaneous and swallowing.

Intuitive Eating

It is a non-diet approach, mind, and body approach to wellness and health. This approach doesn't encourage dieting but emphasizes taking note of the inner body and hunger cues. By trusting our bodies, intuitive healing renews our relationship with food.

Though it doesn't encourage dieting, it uses nutritional information to form healthy eating choices and habits. By this habit, we eat because we'd like to not because we've to, and dietary values are accepted disinterestedly. During this method, we rely more on our intuition. Food is employed to satisfy a requirement. Without the inner cue of hunger, no need for food. Those that want to flee the strain of dieting can appreciate this approach since it's useful and practical. There's no connection between emotions and food during this sort of eating.

Emotional or Stress Eating

It happens when people start overeating or under food once they are overwhelmed with mixed emotions instead of eating in response to their inner cues. Strong emotions we experience can sometimes prevent us from taking note of our physical feelings and thus preventing us from feeling hungry or full.

In such a scenario, food is employed as a mechanism of coping, thus reducing the effect of extreme emotion temporarily. This habit is extremely addictive, and if not controlled, can cause obesity, rapid weight gain, overeating, guilt, and shame.

Stress-related disorder, it cannot handle, can make one vulnerable and not comfortable with the body condition.

This way is where meditation plays a big role because one is going to be ready to handle their stress situation and, therefore, not use food as a coping mechanism.

Stress eating affects many people annually, and although not many will admit it can cause food addiction and unhealthy eating choices. Together eats, they believe diet relieve them of stress and sometimes blame people for their problems. They are doing not take responsibility for their actions.

They do not see the necessity to eat healthy because their mind is preoccupied with numerous things.

Dieting

Dieting only changes the food you eat for a short time and limit your mindset.

Thus, meditation will assist you in tapping into your inner feelings and answering your craving with the power to regulate yourself.

Not being during a diet also causes you to keep your focus because you'll be keen on what you eat and the way beneficial it's to your body. Meditation for weight loss changes the perception of the mind, which successively triggers the inner self to reply to the alternatives and decisions made. Dieting is restrictive and specific on the meals you're to eat.

It challenges the mind to believe that restriction in terms of food is the only path to weight loss. Meditation, however, may be a healthy way of letting the thought be liberal to choose what's best, learn from mistakes, and be ready to specialize in becoming better. It's possible to realize weight loss once one stops the diet process. It offers both future and short-term weight loss needs. However, the disadvantage is you want to know the calories to require per serving. If you are doing not know, you'll take less, and your body is going to be bereft of the needed nutrient.

The Advantage of a Healthy Body

It is essential to take care of a healthy body to take care of achieves a healthy life. A healthy body enables one to steer a lively and more productive life, which directly translates to great achievements and also age gracefully. To take care of a healthy body, one has got to have a healthy diet, subject himself/herself to regular exercises, maintain a stress-free mind, have quality sleep, and also, lead a healthy lifestyle. The subsequent are ten important reasons for maintaining a healthy body.

Boosts the system

A healthy body means all the body processes are performing at their best, and thus all required antibodies for fighting illness are produced in enough amounts. This way, the body can repel diseases and protect the body from getting sick. Albeit the body cannot resist all illnesses, a healthy body is probably going to repel most seasonal illnesses compared to a non-healthy body. It's advised, however, that if the body's system goes down, it's important to avoid consuming alcohol or taking in food and drinks that are sugary as microbes have a high affinity for sugar.

Reduces chances of getting any sort of cancer

A biological explanation is that the disease of cancer is due to the uncontrolled division of cells, caused to a mutation of the DNA within cells. DNA is liable for giving cells instruction on when to divide, what proportion cells to divide, and also repair cells that require repair. When the DNA mutates, the cells divide uncontrollably and do not perform the specified tasks resulting in cancer. Causes of DNA mutations are either inherited genetically, biologically predisposed through chemicals causing disease or unhealthy lifestyles like poor diet, smoking, consumption of loads amounts of alcohol, and obesity. Unhealthy lifestyles are the amount one explanation for cancer. A healthy body contains traditional DNA, which suggests a controlled cellular division and also, proper repair of cells. it's therefore important to take care of a healthy body

Increases the body energy state

A healthy body has high levels of energy, which are as a result of the work put in to realize it—being healthy means having a healthy diet. A healthy diet means the body is furnished with the specified vitamins, carbohydrates, and proteins required. Exercising makes the body adapt to harsh treatment, and reciprocally, every exercise session leaves the frame even stronger than it had been before. Enough sleep clears the mind and also gets obviate fatigue. This compilation ultimately translates to the body having high energy levels and more productive.

Reduces chances of being infertile

Being overweight or underweight can increase one chance of being infertile. Also, the abuse of recreational drugs and smoking can contribute greatly to infertility.

48

Being overweight, smoking, and consuming a lot of alcohol in men reduce the sperm count resulting in infertility. Both being underweight and overweight in women also contributes to infertility. All the above-stated problems are a result of an unhealthy body. Therefore, eating healthy to avoid underweight, exercising to curb obesity and overweight cases, and leading a healthy lifestyle, and minting a healthy body can go an extended way within the cure for infertility.

Prevents stroke and heart-related problems

A stroke is where the brain is bereft of oxygen for a short time, causing death to its cells. Deprivation of oxygen could also be caused by blockage of arteries or rupturing of arteries resulting in leakage of oxygenated blood liable for keeping cells up and running. Among the causes of blocked arteries is thanks to the deposition of fat blocking the right flow of blood to the brain. Other causes may include unhealthy lifestyles and stress. Heart problems include attack and arteria coronaria disease.

Similarly, arteria coronaria disease is caused by an excessive amount of cholesterol, blocking the availability of blood to the body. An attack is that the rapture of the coronary artery; it's as a result of the guts pumping blood at a better rhythmic pressure than the traditional one. This way creates pressure on the artery, causing them to rapture. The simplest treatment approved by doctors for both diseases is exercising, leading a healthy lifestyle, having enough rest, avoiding stress, and also adopting a healthy diet. Doctors stress keeping our bodies healthy as we are ready to repel illnesses like heart problems and stroke, among others.

Enhances some career choices

Careers like athletics require athletes to take care of healthy living standards and impressive body physique. Athletes are required to adopt a strict diet, exercise regularly, and subject their bodies to enough sleep and, most of all, avoid consumption of recreational drugs also as an excessive amount of alcohol if not a little amount. Within the show business, too, models and dancers are mostly required to stick to similar living standards. These healthy standards ensure their bodies are at optimum health, and that they are ready to remain at top of their careers.

Improves longevity

Study within time has shown that having a healthy body ensures one realizes a long life. Exercising as little as twenty minutes each day reduced the probabilities of 1 suffering a premature death. Healthy adjustments like proper diet also are essential in achieving an extended life. A healthy body, even at an older age, also means one is in a position to hold out tasks that might are hard if they were unhealthy or dead. It also means one is in a place to enjoy longer with family. Grandparents get an opportunity to ascertain and bond with their grandchildren all due to maintaining their bodies at healthy levels

Helps control weight

A healthy body may be a state acquired after proper care of the body and exercises. Even without trying to reduce, robust living standards will ultimately cause a healthy weight. A weekly schedule of a couple of hours of training and eating right will go an extended way in maintaining a healthy weight. The body will have a robust system, prevent heart diseases, and also spike the body energy state all as a result of a healthy body

Improves moods and feelings

A study has proven that exercising our body leaves our bodies relaxed and happy also. This way is often a result of the discharge of nerve cell chemicals called endorphins. Training also ensures that one achieves an athletic physique, which suggests that one will have improved physical appearances resulting in enhanced self-confidence. We sleep in a world of constant disappointments and tragedies. it's essential to stay out bodies at the most health for improved emotional balance and also maximum cognitive functions

Helps manage diabetes

There are two primary sorts of diabetes, type one where the body insulin-producing cells are attacked itself, by the body. Then you'll need to survive insulin shots all his/ her life. Type two diabetes is where the body is unable to soak up the sugar within the blood and convert it into energy for the cells. Type one diabetes may be a result of poor health living standards, lack of exercise, and having a poor diet. A correct diet and exercise often control the early stages of diabetes like Pre diabetes and also gestational diabetes. Maintaining a healthy body will mean that the body is going to be ready to control body insulin balance and reduce fatalities caused by diabetes like a vital sign, attack, renal failure, and hardening of blood vessels

Improves the brains memory

A healthy body constitutes a healthy diet; a healthy diet comprises of all the food nutrients. Among these nutrients are vitamins. Vitamins, preferably C, E, D, Omega 3, fatty acids, and flavonoids, are essential in developing a brain with an honest memory. A healthy diet also helps repel dementia and decline of cognitive functions. Dementia is the loss of consciousness that affects the power to talk, think, or maybe solve a drag. Eating healthy will help reduce dementia that isn't caused by physical injury on the brain.

Strengthens the bones and the teeth.

Maintaining a healthy body helps improve the strength of teeth and bones. It's advisable to consume dairy products for calcium three portions each day. One is additionally required to subject the body to physical exercises, and therefore the most preferred one is lifting weights. A correct diet is essential, as well. One is required to consume meals rich in calcium and magnesium for stronger teeth and bones. Many sorts of cereal contain calcium while magnesium is abundantly found in legumes, nuts, whole grains, and seeds

Boosts self-esteem

Among reasons for having low self-esteem has an unhealthy body. We sleep in a world of diversity and one that's rich in several tastes in fashion. Often everyone wants to seem right, but sometimes our bodies often fail us, and this will be bad for our self-esteem. However, this will be changed, and our esteem boosted within no time. A correct diet would be an honest start amid regular body exercises and maintaining a healthy mind through rest and controlling what we expect. Results take time, but eventually, one achieves a healthy body. This way is often more like killing two birds with one stone together is in a position to spice up their self-confidence by enhancing appearances and also achieve a state of a healthy body through having a healthy body.

A Healthy body improves better sleep

Often people with unhealthy bodies undergo tons of difficulties when sleeping. They often sweat tons in cases of obesity and even find problems breathing when asleep. Healthy people sleep well and encounter no problems breathing when sleeping. Subjecting the body to exercises ensures the bodily process work right, and it burns off excess fats causing sweating during the night. Eating right and avoiding abuse of medicine and alcohol also helps achieve a healthy body. A healthy body, in turn, results in sound sleep

Improves sex life in couples

Sex may be a physical act; it's therefore required for both partners to be physically slotted to possess a reasonable time. More often than not, once one among the partners gains an unreasonable amount of weight or both of the partners, they begin experiencing bedroom problems. Sex may be a significant aspect of all couples, and if issues arise during this area, the likelihood of separation is high. It's therefore advised of couples that they maintain healthy bodies to avoid bedroom problems.

Improves chances of surviving disasters and violence

We sleep in the 21st century, where the planet may be a subject of natural disasters also as man inflicted violence's from robbery to wars. The earth is not any longer a secure place, and nobody is an exemption to the present bitter truth. So, just in case of an onset of such misfortunes, the citizenry is alleged to find ways to survive. Among methods of improving the probabilities of survival in such cases has a healthy body, both strong and athletic. The rule of life would take the course, and therefore the strong and fit that healthy people are getting to survive. A healthy person is more likely to evade himself/herself from a scene of violence by moving away as quickly as possible. An unhealthy person won't be so lucky.

Tackling Barriers to Weight Loss

There are numerous barriers to weight loss from personal, to medical, to network and emotional health. Meditation, if incorporated, will bring fruitful and healthy results. Dedication to beat the challenges and to be focused on achieving your goals is critical. There are numerous distractions, especially before you begin your weight loss routine.

It takes discipline and resilience to manage a healthy loss program. We'd like to offer weight loss the priority it deserves. Also, we'd like to understand the existence of the said barriers and their contribution toward our goal. The walls will determine our successes and failures.

Set realistic goals

When you set goals, make sure that they're attainable, specific, and realistic. It's effortless to figure on realistic goals and achieve them for better results. If the goals are unrealistic, the success rate is going to be low and is going to be discouraged. As an example, when starting with meditation, you'll start with as little as five minutes each day and gradually increase it daily until you reach the whole time like sixty minutes.

The same applies to reduce during the meditation process. You'll start that specialize in losing a couple of pounds hebdomadally and gradually increase until you reach your goal. As you set goals, however, realize that it's not your fault if they are doing not compute as you had planned, do your best and keep your focus.

Always be accountable

Once you've got decided to plan meditation for weight loss, don't recoil from sharing your plan with your network and family. It's to make sure that the people you share with also reinforce the commitment and form a part of the system. That way, they're going to feel a part of the program and provides support whenever there's a requirement. You'll also use apps for reminders and timings; in this manner, you've got a backup plan whenever you forget.

You can also use motivational bands whenever you achieve a milestone set. Being accountable causes you to enjoy your successes, acknowledge your failure, and appreciate your network.

People thrive once they feel liable for something, especially on something beneficial to their well-being.

Modify your mindset

Your thinking must be modified within the sense that you simply be keen on the knowledge you're telling yourself. Make sure that your mind isn't crammed with unproductive and negative thoughts, which can bring you down or discourage you. Don't be frightened of challenging your ideas and appreciate your body image.

Your mindset determines your thinking and successively, creates a way of appreciation or rejection. Our weight loss largely depends on our mindset; does one believe you'll do it? If you think that you've got all it takes, then absolutely nothing will prevent or stop you.

Manage stress regularly

Having a stress management technique should be a part of one's daily routine. You would like to develop a healthy stress-relieving mechanism that will assist you in living a stress-free life. Understand that meditation may be a stress reliever in its title because it helps calm the mind and soothes the body.

It is often wont to manage stress and its benefits fully utilized to measure a more productive life. Be ready to handle stress efficiently. The pressure isn't healthy for the mind.

If not handle, it can cause emotional problems and makes one irrational, moody, or violent. Be your boss when managing your stress.

Be educated about weight loss

Suppose you start meditation for weight loss then be educated about how it works; that way, weight loss won't be a struggle.

You will be ready to handle failed attempts also appreciate the progress made.

You will be ready to know what you've got been doing wrong and choose the simplest meditation exercise for you.

If you've got misleading information, then your general progress could also be inhibited

Weight loss needn't be too expensive; neither does it require a costly gym membership or enrolment during a costly meditation class. There are various self-practice meditation exercises that you can comfortably do at the reception. There are multiple meal plans and diets which will work for others though they'll not offer future solutions or lasting behavior changes. Have the proper information that you simply need. Do not be misled by anyone posing that they're professionals therein field. Also, don't hesitate to try to research online and compare notes. From there, you'll be ready to come with something that works for you.

Surround yourself with a network

There are people out there who could also be ready and willing to assist whenever you would like to start out or maybe after you've got started.

The network may include your family, colleagues, friends, or social networks. These groups of wonderful people may encourage and support you to satisfy your long-term goal. After you include them in your plan, they're going to feel accepted, offer opinions, and check on your progress.

Analyze how things are going, also encourage you to continue taking a touch break when necessary.

Your network should also include professionals within the field who will give sound advice and offer needed support and care.

They will also assist you in discovering the items hindering you and holding you behind also as offer reliable information that will help you overcome. As you decide on the professional you would like to figure with, ensure they're people that are easy to speak to. People that are willing to be a participant within the routine you select. You'll also consider people that can give an honest opinion also as recommendations. Support systems sometimes have similar challenges that you simply could even be browsing at that specific time.

Their words of encouragement and best wishes usually would go an extended way in motivating someone. Realize that ideologies may correspond together with your point of view.

Chapter 6. The Importance of Mindful Eating

Mindfulness is a simple concept that states that you must be aware of and present in the moment. Often, our thoughts tend to wander, and we might lose track of the present moment. Maybe you are preoccupied with something that happened or are wondering about something that might happen. When you do this, you tend to lose track of the present. Mindful eating is a practice of being conscious of what and when you eat. It is about enjoying the meal you eat while showing some restraint. Mindful eating is a technique that can help you overcome emotional eating. Not just that, it will teach you to enjoy your food and start making healthy choices. As with any other skill, mindful eating also takes a while to inculcate, but once you do, you will notice a positive change in your attitude toward food. In this, you will learn about a couple of simple tips you can use to practice mindful eating in your daily life.

Reflection

Before you start eating, take a minute and reflect upon how and what you are feeling. Are you experiencing hunger? Are you feeling stressed? Are you bored or sad? What are your wants and what do you need? Try to differentiate between these two concepts. Once you are done reflecting for a moment, you can now choose what you want to eat, if you do want to eat and how you want to eat.

Sit Down

It might save some time if you eat while you are working or while traveling to work. Regardless of what it is, you must ensure that you sit down and eat your meal. Please don't eat on the go, instead set a couple of minutes aside for your mealtime. You will not be able to appreciate the food you are eating if you are trying to multitask.

It can also be quite difficult to keep track of all the food you eat when you are eating on the go.

No Gadgets

If all your attention is focused on the TV, your laptop, or anything else that comes with a screen, it is unlikely that you will be able to concentrate on the meal that you are eating. When your mind is distracted, you tend to indulge in mindless eating. So, limit your distractions or eliminate them if you want to practice mindful eating.

Portion your Food

Don't eat straight out of a container, a bag, or a box. When you do this, it becomes rather difficult to keep track of the portions you eat, and you might overindulge without even being aware of it. Not just that, you will never learn to appreciate the food you are eating if you keep doing this.

Small Plates

We are all visual beings. So, if you see less, your urge to eat will also decrease. It is a good idea to start using small plates when you are eating. You can always go back for a second helping, but this is a simple way to regulate the quantity of food you keep wolfing down.

Be Grateful

Before you dig into your food, take a moment, and be grateful for all the labor and effort that went into providing the meal you are about to eat. Acknowledge the fact that you are lucky to have the meal you do, and this will help create a positive relationship with food.

Chewing

It is advised that you must chew each bite of food at least thirty times before you swallow it. It might sound tedious, but make it a point to chew your food at least ten times before you swallow. Take this time to appreciate the flavors, textures, and taste of the food you are eating. Apart from this, when you thoroughly chew the food before swallowing, it helps with better digestion and absorption of food.

Clean Plate

You don't have to eat everything that you serve on your plate. I am not suggesting that you must waste food. If you have overfilled your plate, don't overstuff yourself. You must eat only what your body needs and not more than that. So, start with small portions and ask for more helpings. Overstuffing yourself will not do you any good, and it is equivalent to mindless eating.

Prevent Overeating

It is important to have well-balanced meals daily. You shouldn't skip any meals, but it doesn't mean that you should overeat. Eat only when you feel hungry and don't eat otherwise. Here are a couple of simple things you can do to avoid overeating. Learn to eat slowly. It isn't a new concept, but not many of us follow it. We are always in a rush these days. Take a moment and slow down. Take a sip of water after every couple of bites and chew your food thoroughly before you gulp it down. Don't just mindlessly eat and learn to enjoy the food you eat. Concentrate on the different textures, tastes, and flavors of the food you eat. Learn to savor every bite you eat and make it an enjoyable experience.

Make your first-bit count and let it satisfy your taste buds. Now is the time to let your inner gourmet chef out! Use a smaller plate while you eat, and you can easily control your portions. Stay away from foods that are rich in calories and wouldn't satiate your hunger. Fill yourself up with foods that can satisfy your hunger and make you feel full for longer. If you have a big bowl of salad, you will feel fuller than you would if you have a small bag of chips. The calorie intake might be the same for both these things, but the hunger you will feel afterward differs. The idea is to fill yourself up with healthy foods before you think about junk food. While you eat, make sure that you turn off all electronic gadgets. You tend to lose track of the food you eat while you watch TV.

Chapter 7. Practicing Hypnosis

We all merely want the time to relax, to fantasy, to fain. It's refreshing to the body and soothing to the soul. As soon as we practice our spirituality, it provides us with only this, a little time to revitalize and enhance our body and mind. The tradition is completed only. It would help if you had a snug and secure location.

A Couple Straightforward Rules

There are several principles to acupuncture, and that they confirm your clinic has become the foremost effective and returns the most superficial benefits. Whenever you're able to start using the sound, locate a snug and secure location in your house or office at which you'll sit, recline, or lie. Ensure that you're comfortable and at a place in which you do not get to look closely at anything. Don't hear a trance work as you're driving a vehicle or operating any kind of machine. It's helpful to settle on a typical time every day or nighttime to exercise your self-hypnosis. Bedtime may be a fantastic chance to please in your trance work. Practicing now could also be an excellent means to place in a comfy sleep.

Distractions are unavoidable. As against letting them frighten you and take you aside from the trancework, use them. Use the noises from the environment around you to enhance your trance encounter. For instance, while performing your hypnosis, you'll hear noise and start believing this noise is distracting you. You become more concentrated with this diversion in your hypnosis. You'll be enticed to fight against it, which takes away energy in the hypnosis. Instead, once you hear a noise that initially sounds distracting or annoying, treat this by providing it together with your consent to be there due to ground noise.

Give it a mission, like thinking to yourself that "the noise of the barking dog is assisting you in moving deeper and deeper inside," or even "the fan engine appears to be a waterfall that's soothing ground noise ."

At our practice at Tucson, there is a day school that necessarily lets out the youngsters play through one among their hypnosis sessions. That's once we indicate, "The noise of youngsters might be a ground noise which allows you to maneuver deeper and deeper inside yourself. "This may be a portion of the "usage everything" doctrine. Distractions also incorporate the senses you'll experience inside you. For instance, you would possibly find yourself discovering a neighborhood of your body which itches. The more you consider the itching or scratching the itch, the less you focus your awareness about the trance. Sometimes, you remind yourself that you've got permission to transfer your focus back to your state or daydream and permit the itch to maneuver unscratched. When handling individuals with pain ailments, we instruct them to concentrate attention away in the "diversion" of annoyance in a similar manner. We will not control the environment around the senses in us, but we could pick where we concentrate our attention.

If you've problems letting go of a bothersome distraction, you will get to control the backdrop noise or feeling, allowing you to move more smoothly in. Detach yourself from whatever that's distracting your focus from your hypnosis. Hand over any battle with the environment. Only make it there, and sooner or later, you'll not detect it if you find out how to require a sense, sound, or another component that interferes together with your hypnosis. You do not let it get control over you.

Law of Reversed Effect

There's a law in mediation, referred to as the Law of Reversed Effect, which states that the longer you plan to do anything, the longer it doesn't occur. A real example is that if you'd wish to convey a reputation, you recognize you understand--it could be a book title, a private, a picture--but you cannot say it immediately. Therefore, the longer you attempt, the less it's there. The title comes once you inform a subconscious thought that "I will remember after," or "It will come to me afterward." By letting go of this question, you've introduced your subconscious thoughts to regain and supply the response, and it always will. The Law of Reversed Effect is that it merely provides you with the reverse (the opposite) whenever you're trying too difficult to get something.

Simple Techniques

Getting absorbed into your ideas and thoughts is a gentle trip to the center of self-known as "entering a trance." The natural self-hypnosis methods contain entering trance, broadening the ecstasy, providing suggestions and messages into this mind-body, and coming from the rapture.

Moving Into Trance

Whenever you're employing the trancework about the sound, it'll become your guide once you enter a trance. I'll use a trance induction procedure; you'll discover focusing and relaxing. You've likely noticed the swinging view approach in films. However, there are many unique methods to focus you specialize in entering the trance. You'll stare at an area on the wall, then use a breathing procedure, or use innovative body comfort. You'll hear various induction approaches on the trancework sound.

They're only the clues or the signs which you're committing to saying, "I'm entering trance" or even "I will perform my negativity today." getting into trance can also be considered as "permitting yourself to daydream... intentionally". You're letting yourself become consumed with your ideas, eradicated, and allowing yourself to pretend or imagine what you would like as real and achieved. There's no "going under." Instead, there is a beautiful experience of moving inside.

Deepening The Trance

Deepening your trance makes it possible to become more absorbed into your mind, thoughts, and expertise. It is often through with innovative comfort, heading "deeper and deeper inside." With scenes or images, or only by simply counting a couple of chains. We like to indicate that you produce a vertical vision connected with moving deeper, including a path leading to a hill or a lush green valley as you hear the counting right down to zero. Since you listen to me, you'll envision or imagine going deeper into a spectacle or location that's even easier and enjoyable to you. that's what we mean by "deepening the trance."

Talking Into the Mind of Your Own Body with Messages and Tips

Throughout the trancework, you'll hear your voice lecture two components of your mind. One portion of your brain is that the conscious mind thoughts. That is the part of you who is great at telling the time, making change, and understanding how to write and skim. It's "thinking thoughts." Through the trancework, your believing thoughts will keep it up, performing its regular getting ideas. So that you do not get to be worried about clearing your head, or draining your head, or placing your mind entirely asleep.

Just see your thoughts will last "believing," and your task is to disconnect or unplug merely enough, so you do not get to answer those notions. You permit them to flow by.

If your "to-do" list keeps shooting up, for instance, simply let it flow by rather than life thereon. I will be lecturing you about another portion of the mind that we predict your subconscious thoughts --"sub" since it's under your belief degree of consciousness. It's that the "mind of the physique." Your subconscious has the knowledge to handle your body's trillions of cells, your body chemistry, and every one of the body's acts of breathing, digestion, and therefore the system, the system, and also the system.

The mind-body features a massive quantity of wisdom. Also, in performing your hypnosis, you're amassing and obtaining additional knowledge your own body's thoughts will influence, according to your motivation, your own beliefs, alongside your expectations, and assist you together with your weight reduction.

This tailoring procedure is essential. It must suit you personally since it is your self-hypnosis, and every one of the hypnosis is self-hypnosis. As we've mentioned, hypnosis isn't something to you. It's something you're being advised to encounter, and since you discover it, you're learning it. Repeating and rehearsal produce strong knowledge and skill inside you.

Perhaps you'll call it unconscious understanding as your subconscious might take it bent you without you wanting to consider it. The ideas that could bother you about your weight loss are presently shifted into something that supports your ideal body—alongside your mind-body. For instance, if you think you are a more "yo-yo" dieter since you've always recovered the load you've lost.

You would possibly use your trancework to point, "Every single day I'm losing weight, alongside my entire body, remembers the way to make this a lasting ability. I'm achieving my ideal weight". Subconscious comprehension or maybe the mind-body wisdom learned from the trancework is far like choosing to ride a motorcycle or drive a vehicle. There seemed to be many things to seem closely at precisely an equivalent time when you're learning. However, quite fast, your hard-won on this understanding so that you'll be ready to drive. And you do not even get to inform your toes precisely what to do.

Coming from Trance

At the close of the trancework sessions, you'll hear me talking about allowing your body to awaken with a way of refreshment and wellbeing. Also, bringing this refreshment with you into the surface of the mind, so you come from trance feeling renewed and awake. Or, when performing your hypnosis at night, you would possibly drift into a deep, relaxed sleep. Once you're alert, it's crucial to debrief.

Here is that the opportunity to make a note or two on your ideas or thoughts that came to mind will be handy to you. Frequently during childbirth, you are not just providing messages into your own body, but also your body is chatting with you, and you will be taking note of your body's thoughts.

Your body can reveal quite beneficial info, and you would possibly prefer to write it all down. As an example, let's suppose you have a selected food which you only cannot resist, a meal like french-fried potatoes, which was the "downfall" of dieting. Throughout the trancework, you would possibly find an insight (something you noticed once you listened to the brain of your own body) that allows you to know french-fried potatoes became an obstruction or a "relaxation" for you mentally.

That insight today permits you to select what you'd like instead of only execute the prior pattern, which has been established for possibly decades ago and created from a subjective experience that's way back and no more legitimate in your lifetime.

Jennifer was meticulous and hardworking in each area of her life, alongside virtually every aspect of her burden loss program. She exercised daily, ate much produce, drank much water, loved grains, and purchased organic material. She made quite wise decisions for wellness but stayed twenty pounds in her ideal weight.

As she sat in our workplace, she told her insatiable appetite for frozen dessert (natural though it had been) every evening and in each social opportunity that presented itself. Throughout her trancework, we inquired if there had been a component of her, why she seemed to crave frozen dessert. She had been quiet for several moments, then reiterated the long-ago words of her adoring grandfather: "Jenny, beloved, frozen dessert would be the perfect reward for hard labor, so she consumes while it continues. "After she discovered the origin of her ice hockey lotion urge, she managed to understand it but not finish it often.

What Was the Experience Like for You?

Now that you've had experience using self-hypnosis, what did you encounter? Are you currently "hypnotized"? are you able to attend a hypnotic trance? Nearly all folks that are new to hypnosis will ponder whether they experienced it. You would possibly feel precisely an equivalent. If you were anticipating a profoundly changed state of awareness, then you've found that there's no "going under" without a loss of awareness. You recognize where you were, what you're doing, if not all the instant.

We hear an equivalent testimony whenever people have finished their initial encounter with self-hypnosis: "This was wonderful (or amazing, or exceptional, or impressive)."

When I'm asked what I encounter in a trance, my school years' clear image comes into mind. When I had been looking outside the window during a lecture. I would not understand what the professor was lecturing, but I'd hear his voice. However, I did not have any idea what he had been saying through those minutes. Being trance is extremely almost like being in a daydream country. The many difference between a trance and a daydream is that a state may be a deliberate quiet daydream wherein you're consumed in thoughts that you simply need your mind-body to debate. When in mind, you experience an aim to provide your mind-body with suggestions or ideas about what you'd love it to do to you personally.

We're always thrilled to listen to folks say following their very first trance encounter, "I enjoyed it. I didn't want it to finish." We understand that when a seasoned trance is found, they might take action.

Hypnotic Phenomena

Trance may be a delicate experience. You'll examine the subtleties of what you believed, what you discovered, not discovering, and what you've experienced. Some could feel heavy, their legs and arms might be immovable, or they could feel mild, weightless, or maybe drifting. Some may feel cool or warm or be absorbed in the emotional imagery they desire they're in their vision. Regions of the physical body may appear to fade so wholly they are not even detected. It is also common to experience a while. One minute might seem as if ten minutes or ten minutes might sound like only one. Of these are ordinary experiences, we predict "hypnotic phenomena."

If you're conversant with daydreaming, you recognize that a lot of what is referred to as hypnotic phenomena also can be common waking-state phenomena. How frequently have you ever "awakened" of a daydream, or maybe been roused from an intriguing book or film, to get that a surprising quantity of your time has elapsed? The available array of happenings with misuse is extensive, like hyperalgesia (the decrease in pain) and also hypoesthesia (the removal of annoyance). When in a trance, an individual may imagine a neighborhood or all her body is indeed readily numb that she will undergo surgery using hypnosis because of the only anesthetic.

You'll be pleased to understand those hypnotic phenomena that might be generated, especially helpful for weight reduction. You'll have the power to make, for instance, a physical feeling of fullness, or maybe a looking for wholesome food. You'll have the ability to make sense of improved taste or odor. You would possibly even have the power to overlook foods that are not according to your weight reduction objectives. You would possibly even be surprised to feel a looking for the exercise. Bear in mind the power of self-hypnosis. It's possible to pick what you'd wish to convey for your mind-body. It's possible to settle on what you would like your mind-body to perform for you. It is your option, your ideal weight.

Shrink Stomach Without Surgery

Before discovering malnutrition, obesity, a heart condition, and a spread of disorders that affect the physical body, people eat what they need stupidly about what percentage calories and inadequate nutrition they put in their stomachs. But with the changing lifestyle, people are more concerned about their health and therefore the effects of obesity.

Weight loss surgery isn't new, although many of our friends have had surgeries to reduce, and it's been a trend for a short time. But most of those surgeries are a short-term solution to losing weight.

One of the common surgeries that always help overweight people is the gastric bypass. More specifically, restrictive gastric bypass, bariatric gastric bypass, and the laparoscopic gastric band are the most common. Restrictive gastric bypass involves attaching an adjustable gastric band to the stomach and reducing food intake without affecting the digestive process. On the opposite hand, the bariatric gastric bypass puts a hollow band around the stomach and forms a small pouch and a skinny passage that results in the stomach's remaining part. You'll always feel full once you have this procedure. The laparoscopic gastric band is a smaller amount of invasive and uses a band through and around the stomach. If you set adjustable straps around your belly, you get a smaller stomach. The result's almost like a bariatric bypass for gastroplasty that restricts food intake.

Although many doctors support these methods to reduce overweight patients, there's still a risk of surgery and are concerned about pre-and postoperative complications and difficulties in adapting to their new diet. One of these operations is often fatal and irreversible. Before you opt, consult your doctor, family, and discuss your options with them. Losing weight is usually achieved patiently, with perseverance, self-control, and diligence. Even surgery doesn't offer a long-term solution but is merely temporary.

Losing weight with exercise and the right nutrition can help you achieve the body and health you usually wanted. Come to me to realize your goal of losing weight!

Can you reduce the dimensions of your stomach without gastric bypass surgery? The solution is yes. Gastric surgery changes your stomach's size through staples, ligaments, or other surgical changes to the stomach. Limit the quantity of food you'll eat by restricting your stomach to a smaller container. In bands, your belly grows as big as a ball. You certainly want to be leaner, and surgery seems like a moment fix, but don't need to save lots of all of your money by not doing this surgery and trying to assist yourself by shrinking your stomach? In any case, you made it as big by putting as much food in your mouth as you wanted. The skin is elastic and stretches to the dimensions it grows. Your stomach is additionally flexible, expanding to any size that corresponds to the quantity of food you eat. The other is also true: your stomach will shrink to soak up the amount of food you set in it.

What is the particular shape of your stomach? It's approximately twelve inches long and 6 inches wide at its widest point. It channels your food after it's been digested in the upper alimentary canal, where it's processed into fuel for your body. If your body has enough power to stay you going, excess energy is stored in your body as fat and cellulose. How big can your stomach stretch? Check out a gallon container of water. A gallon of water weighs a minimum of eight pounds. One gallon is adequate for sixteen cups. Your stomach is often stretched to accommodate a minimum of a gallon, and with a daily overhead diet at every meal, it is often extended to gigantic sizes.

Also, take a glance at a quart container. There are quite two pounds of 1 liter of water and 4 cups of water. This way is often large enough to incorporate enough food in a typical meal to strengthen your body and store excess fat and cellulose.

Two cups of food are quite sufficient to satisfy your needs in one meal. Attempt to measure the food you set on your plate. Put your usual amount of food on your plate, then measure everything. Write this amount down. You'll be amazed at the quantity of food you eat. The rationale you feel like eating is that your body needs fuel to figure, play, walk, and exercise. Are you sure you would like to spend the hard-earned money on surgery? There are some ways to scale back the dimensions of your stomach.

Eat small, frequent meals.

Your stomach won't stay big if you do not keep it full. It'll slowly shrink to the dimensions you would like for the food you get. By gradually reducing your stomach a day, you maintain a sense of fullness. After all, the stomach features a big screaming voice and may look out of its needs. Rather than overflowing this gallon-sized container, you'll satisfy it by thoroughly chewing every bite of food very slowly. Did you recognize that it takes twenty minutes for your stomach to send a message to your brain that it's reached the full mark? Twenty minutes may be a while to continue eating. You would like to hurry up the news broker. Without a doubt, your express runner carries tons of fat and may hardly reach the brain to press the stop-eating button.

So now you have a drag. You do not know when to prevent eating, and you almost certainly hate when your stomach cramps with emptiness. The simplest solution to the present problem is to chew slowly. Chew every bite. They will be devoured as quickly as you'll shovel. For soft foods, you ought to consume in small bites. Try eating with a baby spoon that mothers feed their babies with. Sounds funny. You're trying to satisfy your stomach to the complete, and you've to place the inside track down.

Meat and other solid foods should be chewed a minimum of 40 times. You do not need to count; just chew until your food is nearly like mashed potatoes. You cannot drown like that.

Your stomach needs fluid to digest food. Then drink when eating is the way how to feel fresh. Take a bite to eat, chew it alright, and wash it down with many glasses of water. Don't worry; not all nutrients are going to be far away from the food. All vitamins and nutrients are processed in your lower alimentary canal.

You are what you eat. Your stomach size is the size you permit. Less food means fewer calories than you consume, and fewer calories end in a loss of body mass. This fact is often not a fast fix. It took an extended time to get older, but if you chew slowly in at some point and eat many small meals, you'll be faster than you think that.

Scrummy Tummy may be a safe and effective method of losing weight. There are different names and variations on this method, but all of them use the facility of their minds to convince you that your stomach is smaller.

This way is a hypnotic way to shrink your belly by going back through a virtual gastric band or hypnotic band so you'll reap the advantages without the pain, risk, and tremendous cost of actual surgery.

Here you'll find more details about your selection:

Costly and painful surgery?

Tailor-made hypnosis session package that guides you to your ideal weight and size

Virtual gastric band surgery with abdominoplasty or hypnotic lap band weight management can help you achieve your goals, look leaner, and more attractive.

Just as a correct operation isn't for everyone, here are some ways you'll decide which one is true for you. I'm a hypnotic weight loss professional, not a doctor, so I will be able to specialize in sharing what I do know to assist you in creating the right decision for yourself.

You must be open-minded and prepared to make these changes for the hypnotic virtual gastric band method (either personal guided image sessions or the audio program package). Does one want the results? Does one feel comfortable with the increased positive attention you get once you are slimmer and appear more attractive or feel more beautiful? Believe it or not, some who are overweight have unconscious reasons to remain heavy.

If you simply want to reduce what people are saying or thinking, this is often not the simplest option. The critical changes come from in, and you would like these advantages for YOU! Often your self-image changes first from the in. This way helps you to see and feel the way you would like from the surface.

However, if you're open and need to require advantage of this method and regain control of your diet and weight, you'll be pleasantly surprised at how effective this method is going to be for you. It's possible that in a few months after you've reached your ideal size and weight and are satisfied with the results, you'll maintain an appearance back on this perfect naturally and easily. a choice you've made now!

The shrunken belly is like pictures. You'll imagine the dimensions of the littlest stomach and see how a smaller stomach means you eat less.

You also feel full earlier, and when days become weeks and weeks become months, your weight and height change, and you become leaner. You'll see, feel and picture yourself as a leaner who eats less, and thus your subconscious will follow this plan and assist you in designing your new image.

Best of all, you'll keep this new weight and size because your self-image has been redesigned. Your subconscious is going to be given the right image and style of your body if you feed your body with the proper nutrition.

Shedding Pregnancy Pounds Quickly With Hypnosis

Bringing a toddler into the planet can cause you to very happy. This motherhood phase is probably one of the simplest moments for a lady. However, the results aren't equivalent, especially if you would like to travel back to your previous stature and reduce. How can you find the time to obviate the load you gained during your pregnancy with a replacement baby?

You may consider diets and workouts, but you're likely limited in time because the baby is your priority. Besides, enormous efforts are needed to get through it. As this is often the matter for many women who wish to lose pregnancy-related weight, they have to be offered clear weight loss programs.

Luckily, a number of the load gained during pregnancy was shown to decrease through hypnosis. It acts very similar to treatment in that you'll reduce without having to struggle too hard in a matter of weeks. But you'll also relax and reduce the strain in your body due to all the stress.

With hypnosis, you'll devote longer to your baby instead of in the gym. There is no got to believe what food you'll eat. It's because hypnosis allows you to pick the simplest food without knowing you're deprived. Hypnosis can potentially be a healthy weight loss device.

Hypnosis can also motivate you to combat impulsive food, one of the triggers for weight gain. It is often stressful to take care of your weight, particularly once you need to reduce your appetite. You will not need to suffer under hypnosis, with the advantage of losing weight on the way.

If you're worried about increasing numbers due to pregnancy on the weighing scale display, there's no got to worry. Returning to make won't be a drag with hypnosis. With this approach, you'll now lose your pregnancy and spend more precious moments together with your newborn boy.

Chapter 8. How to use meditation and affirmations to lose weight?

The practice of meditation centers the mind on calmness and clarity. This allows you to handle tension, which, in most situations, raises your appetite and encourages you to eat unconsciously. We also use weight as they want to make their food comfortable. While there isn't much research that directly shows that meditation helps you lose weight, meditation helps you become more conscious of what you think and do, including food. Meditation can help both with food and emotion.

There are many ways to meditate, but most meditation types have some common things; a quiet place to meditate, a relaxed setting with reduced chances of distractions. A particular position, such as sitting, sitting, standing, or walking, is comfortable and natural for you; a concentration on an expression, phrase, breath, or something else.

A Focus of Attention

You have to concentrate on one thing that will steal your time. If you are an open mind, other thoughts are natural while meditating, so try not to become too involved. Continue to concentrate your attention back on your breath, sentence, or whatever. Select your place, time, and process. Meditation calls for a commitment to stop and look in and around you, even if you only have a few moments.

Do not try to offer great expectations, but let them unfold unchecked. Most people have an inner critic who lives. To reframe your thinking, you know what's working for you when you wake up and wake up again at the end of the day.

We get so cooked up and don't spend time looking around and seeing what is good. One of the daily tasks takes 30 seconds to look and see what lies ahead. This is a way to stay.

You don't just have to be present right now, but you must make the right decisions; what to eat, what to avoid, and the best exercises for someone with high blood pressure and lifestyle choices? This is called intelligent comprehension. Meditation does not substitute for diet, exercise, and following the weight loss and better blood pressure guidelines of your doctor. However, if you do it with patience and commitment, you can support those positive changes.

We are conscious of psychological wellbeing and meditation, but how do you change your fat and improve your weight, losing it? The response is the psychological factors of gaining weight and eating behavior. Over time, multiple studies showed sensitivity to decreased binge consumption, emotional consumption, and weight loss. Here are some more details on how carefulness can help you lose fat and weight.

Have you tried to lose weight and failed? If so, you know how tough a weight loss program can be to stick to, and though you do drop these extra pounds, it's another fight together to hold them off. However, you don't have to waste the rest of your life struggling with your will to stay lean.

One of the biggest differences between those who lose weight and excel in holding it away is that the previous group changes the way they eat and work and the way they think.

In reality, if you do not have your mind on your side, it will be difficult or impossible to lose weight because you constantly sabotage yourself. Let's look at the kind of thinking that leads to a continuous, healthy weight loss.

Carefulness

First of all, you must be careful. Many that slowly and gradually lose weight would most likely hold it off. Forget all those diets which guarantee that you can lose 10 pounds or more in a week, most of which are water weight, and will be recovered as soon as you begin to eat regularly.

It is just human to want a fast fix, but it is worth taking a gradual approach if you want to lose weight, keep your life off and keep up without continuously battling the rest of your life with your body because cuts make weight loss more difficult and time-consuming over the long term.

Versatility

For effective long-term weight loss, versatility is also essential. You can lose weight, but it may be that you would be unhappy if you make overly strict rules for what you can and can't eat and are unable to adhere to those rules in your lifetime and if you have this kind of 'all or nothing' mentality, and break-even a little your rules, it may be tempting to do a whole binge after that because after all, you have blown it now!

If, on the other hand, you follow sensitive guidelines while recognizing that when you consume foods that are not part of your daily diet, often (such as holidays and special occasions), these 'forbidden foods' appear less desirable since they aren't something which you have forbidden from your life forever.

Consistency

Consistency is another aspect of a good weight loss regime. This may seem to contradict the above point, but it doesn't. The main thing is that you eat healthily and, most of the time, obey your workout schedule. You will also stop youthful and unhealthy habits, such as the binge/starve period.

The behavior you take most of the time provides you with the outcome you want. Instead of pursuing a fast solution, you will be more driven to follow a moderate, balanced approach that you will regularly execute when you are committed to making long-term lifestyle improvements.

Respect for oneself

It is also important to be optimistic about yourself. If you are like most people who try to lose weight, you would probably not feel very positive about your body and appearance. While you don't have to pretend to love anything you don't like about yourself, it is also important not to continually beat yourself because you're not at your goal.

If you are one of the people who appear to overheat in reaction to stress, such self-recrimination would possibly make you feel even worse and more vulnerable to survival - which means that the vicious cycle gets worse.

Try focusing on what you do and if you have days when you skip training or do not eat as much as you want, take care not to judge yourself too harshly. Instead, understand that it happens to everybody and do your best just to start again. You just need a moderate regime that is good enough; note that you do not have to eat or practice perfectly to lose weight.

If you can make these things part of your daily thinking, it should be easier to lose weight. However, it can be challenging, especially if you have a poor attitude and weight loss efforts. One thing that will motivate you to pursue more empowered thinking is to use a meditation recording of weight loss.

Use a consistency record that includes brainwave training technology. You will potentially gain easier access and use basic tools like affirmations and visualization to reprogram it with new values that work against you.

Such recordings involve repeated sounds of certain frequencies that make entering a profoundly relaxed and focused state easier for your brain. In this state, the subconscious is more open to suggestions, and any reinforcement or visualization work you do is better. This is an effective way to improve your mind from the inside, even though you are not familiar with meditation or other mind control methods.

It is worth the little effort that it takes to do this because it is so much easier to make positive changes in your life, including losing weight, if your mind is on your side. You do not need to rely on a willingness to combat your self-destruction drive – because those forces are simply no longer there.

'Improve the Inner You' and Lose Weight!

Open your mind to the chance your body is unbelievable and willing to do amazing things. Going beyond basic mental and physical fitness requires cultivating and improving the 'inner self' to be balanced. It is important to lose weight, but it's easier to lose weight if you feel more inside. Here are some perfect ways to reconnect with your inner self.

Connectivity

Get to know people. Don't waste the entire time on the internet socially. The research showed that less than 4 to 6 friends cause problems, particularly with colds and other illnesses in your body systems. This is because isolation can make you more vulnerable to illness and cause chemical changes in your body.

Nature

Living in the world today, you can easily forget that salmon came from the sea, not from your local supermarket. You have to go out, and I don't mean the pay-TV channel 'Discovery.'

Research has shown that your well-being relies on a deep friendship with nature. You must see nature as a valuable resource; don't take it for granted. The only way to do this is to dive into it. Smell the flowers, take a natural stroll, run in the park, or visit an aquarium.

Look in the sky and see the precious things called stars without thought at all, enjoy them. You will boost your mental alertness, focus, and cognitive efficiency by appreciating and immersing yourself in nature. Do not take nature as a matter of course; it's not just the enjoyment of nature; it's the connection.

Meditation

You practice meditation to pay attention to your own body, be present at the moment, and practice your inner self's art. Meditation has been recommended to improve stress by relieving muscle stress, reducing breathing rates, helping with the heart rate and blood pressure, increasing immunity, and rest.

Meditation is so diverse that there would be the right type for you. Try some different shapes and choose the one you want. This way, you are more likely to continue the meditation practice daily. Many times during the day, you can practice meditation, e.g., walking, fall asleep, or just breathe deeply; it does not have to take very long to practice daily.

Follow your hobbies

A hobby gives you imagination and the chance to explore a new side. Studies have shown that lobbying or interested people have a more optimistic attitude, are less nervous and less depressed, and make you happier and healthier. When selecting a hobby, make sure that it's complicated and interesting enough, but not too difficult, to frustrate you. By the way, it's not a hobby to watch TV! Try a new hobby and get 'hooked' today!

There are so many long-standing advantages of looking after the "inner" you can make yourself happier and healthier by taking time off and making time. Doing any or all of the above allows you to lose weight and be a confident and 'fresher' person on the inside.

It's like cleaning your car but keeping the inside dirty. It gets you down every time you get into the car, but if both inside and outside is clean, you get a sense of wow' – that's awesome! Our bodies are no different from the inside and outside of your car.

There is mostly a link between weight troubles and low self-esteem. The reasons can be complex, however, people with low shallowness regularly are seeking consolation or solace in food. Or, they may lack the discipline needed to appear after themselves and have low shallowness. However, with a paltry attempt, your shallowness can be improved.

In most cases, we form our feelings of self-esteem through our research experiences in childhood. If you weren't credible to love and respect yourself, then you probably go through low self-esteem. The first rule of getting to know to like and respect yourself is to banish bad self-communication from your vocabulary.

Self-criticism is destructive. Your unconscious mind accepts the things you say unconditionally. If you are forever berating yourself for being foolish, all you are doing is programming yourself to feel that way. Remember, whatever you repeatedly affirm will become self-fulfilling.

After eliminating self-criticism from your inner dialogue, you can learn to love and respect yourself more by focusing on your successes. Being a wonderful parent to your children is a major success in life and all too often very overlooked. Being compassionate and generous are also wonderful traits that most people possess. If you have ever received or executed anything, however small, don't be afraid to praise yourself. Maybe you're doing nicely at work, or you've executed a private aim. Always examine what you have completed, acknowledge it, and be happy with yourself. There is nothing wrong with praising and being proud of yourself-—it is something you should embrace. Use the learning to love yourself.

Eliminate Negative Self-Talk

Never, ever speak negatively to yourself. This can be so destructive. If you repeat something frequently enough, your unconscious mind will soon accept it as a fact. So, if you often berate yourself by calling yourself stupid or useless, you're programming yourself terribly. You will then unconsciously respond to that poor programming and in reality create situations for yourself that make you sense silly or useless.

Remember the computer analogy—what your program is what will come returned out. The human thoughts are exactly like that, so any more you must in no way vocally or internally say (or even think) terrible matters approximately yourself. I understand this is not usually clean if you have had a lifetime of bad conditioning and your shallowness is low, however, you need to begin fresh from this second. By reprogramming your "laptop" with effective ideals about yourself, over time you may construct more self-belief and vanity. It is a case of "fake it till you make it."

From now on view your errors and mistakes as matters that will educate you about something. Look for the lesson within the error, but stop punishing or berating yourself. Sometimes we analyze the most important lessons via our errors. The key is to research the lesson so you don't make the identical mistake once more and hold your self-belief by preserving a wonderful inner dialogue. Admire your approach regularly to help you build your vanity.

LEARN TO LOVE yourself completely, faults and all. When you sincerely love and appreciate yourself, you open yourself up to being loved and revered with the aid of others. Cultivate the habit of loving yourself via acknowledging your achievements and specialize more in your excellent points.

Close your eyes, take some deep breaths, and loosen up. Take a few moments to clean away any unwanted mind and allow your thoughts to turn out to be still. Then cognizance on all the petty matters that you have done in your lifestyles—any genuine work you've done, any accurate friendships you've cultivated, anything you've received or praised for. Keep your recognition of all the positives in your lifestyles and experience, in reality, desirable about yourself as you do so.

Enhance or even exaggerate all the feelings and photos by making them big, bright, and very clear. Be pleased with yourself as you try this and repeat the following affirmations:

- I love and respect myself.

- I am proud of myself.

- My vanity is strong.

Repeat the affirmations over and over like a slow mantra, saying the words with total belief and genuine conviction. This is an excellent exercise to put powerful feelings into, but make sure you remain deeply relaxed at the same time. Draw these words deep inside you so they resonate with you.

Continue this technique regularly over several days until you feel your self-esteem growing strong.

As your self-esteem grows, your desire to improve the quality of your life and be healthy will also grow stronger. When your self-esteem is strong, you will only want to do things well for your well-being. You won't want to load your body up with fattening food, vegetate in front of the TV every night, or let your body become bloated and out of shape. Instead, you will have an inner desire that drives you to make positive changes and improve all aspects of your life. You will also naturally gravitate toward other people who believe in themselves and who have positive aims.

When you build strong self-esteem and a disciplined approach toward your eating and exercise habits, it is easy to connect with like-minded people. Your outer life is often a reflection of your inner thoughts and feelings. So look around you. If you don't like what you see, make the changes from within and things will soon change around you. You have the free will to make changes, and with less effort and discipline, you will do just that.

If there are issues from your past connected to weight control that have held you back, make a vow to yourself to achieve your weight loss goal despite the past. Don't hold on to any anger against those who contributed to your low self-esteem and weight problems. This is a waste of energy. If you believe other people have caused you to suffer and you hold on to the anger, those same people still have power over you. All this anger does is continue to hold you back.

Use the releasing techniques if you need to let go of any negativity or anger relating to the past. If you need further help, seek out a well-qualified hypnotherapist. When looking for a hypnotherapist for a one-on-one session, call some, and find someone you feel snug with. Check that the person's qualifications are from a well-established body and ask for references and proof of insurance if you feel the need. Wonderful therapy is all about dynamics between the therapist and client. So finding a therapist who inspires you and who can get to the root of any problem is the key to successful therapy.

No matter what, never give up on letting go of negativity and anger because hanging on to negative emotions will only slow your progress. The positive self-image technique will help your self-image. Once again, you are aiming to program your mind with a new belief, which it will automatically respond to.

Positive Self-Image Technique

CLOSE YOUR EYES. Breathe slowly and deeply until your mind is still and you feel very relaxed. Then imagine yourself as you want to be. Create a picture of the perfect you standing in front of you, full of confidence and self-belief. See the confident way this self-assured you stand and how you hold yourself. Make the picture very positive, bright, and clear.

Now, step into your perfect self and imagine you are looking out through your own eyes. Connect with the positive feelings and notice how good you feel in your perfect self. Amplify the pleasant emotions and affirm they will stay with you in your everyday lifestyles.

Practice this technique regularly, especially when your confidence and self-esteem need a boost.

Positive Modeling

As human beings, we often seek to validate the weaknesses of our behavior and unpleasant habits. It is frequently the case that people choose friends who have similar unhealthy habits because it allows them to feel okay about their behaviors. If you're twenty-5 pounds obese and you've got buddies, forty pounds overweight, it could be clean to justify your excesses by saying, "I'm now not as horrific as so and so."

Now I'm not saying you should dump all your overweight or unhealthy friends! But don't judge yourself against others who are weak-willed and content to stay stuck. Rather, you must aspire to model yourself after people who are fit and healthy, if that is what you want.

The brief Neuro-Linguistic Programming (NLP) modeling technique will help you learn to absorb and assimilate the same qualities held by someone who inspires you.

Neuro-linguistic Programming is a therapeutic tool for effective communication, goal setting, influencing, sped up learning, and behavior modification. It can help you model your behavior on a positive example. It is as though you are absorbing the habits of the person in question and then importing these positive characteristics into your consciousness.

Imagine a friend, relative, or acquaintance you know who eats healthily, exercises regularly, and has a body shape and size that you aspire to. If you can't think of anyone who fits the bill, imagine a famous super-fit athlete whom you admire.

When someone comes to thoughts, be aware of this man or woman as a version of your method to weight reduction and fitness. Imagine his or her healthy eating plans and fitness routines, and embrace this person's positive habits for your aims. Read the NLP modeling script a few times until you know what to do and then practice this technique whenever you need inspiration.

Neuro-Linguistic Programming Modeling for Weight Loss Technique

CLOSE YOUR EYES and allow yourself to become comfortable. Breathe very slowly and deeply, in through your nostril and out through your mouth. Make each breath long and deep, and relax increasingly more with every slow breath exhaled.

Now, focus on someone who is very fit and healthy and who inspires you. Preferably it should be a person you know and see fairly often, but if no one comes to mind, focus on a famous athlete. It must be a person you admire for being very fit and healthy, not someone who is reasonably fit and healthy. Set a lofty goal for this technique.

Take a moment to see this person in your mind's eye, and focus on his or her level of health and fitness. Just focus on the qualities and everything that you like about this person. Take a moment to feel very inspired.

Now imagine that these qualities are becoming part of you. Feel as though you are drawing this person's determination and discipline deep inside yourself. Imagine you are absorbing and assimilating the same very positive, single-minded attitude toward your health and well-being. Make these traits a part of you now.

Next, visualize yourself-reaching your fitness aim with the identical self-belief and resolution as the character you admire. You are in control of your weight now and determined to become and remain fit, toned, and healthy in the same way this person has. Take a moment to focus on this. Be creative and use all of your senses when you visualize yourself expressing the new characteristics that will help you achieve and maintain great fitness.

Take all the time you want to do this. When you are ready to finish, permit your thoughts to clear and slowly count from one to three. Open your eyes and come again to full waking consciousness.

Be creative when you use this technique and practice it regularly!

One thing to note is that if the person you are modeling ever goes off the rails and gains weight, this will not happen to you because you are modeling only his or her positive traits.

Banishing Negativity

Never let self-doubt or negativity get in your way. Negative thoughts are a part of what makes us human — the secret is not to dwell on them. Whenever you get a negative thought, just let it drift away and refocus on the positive.

Be aware of how the media can be a negative influence. Television and radio advertisers know how to manipulate you and sometimes walk a fine line with the use of mood music and persuasive language, especially in food advertising. It seems every other TV ad is a junk food ad or an ad featuring a warm, compassionate-looking actor selling drugs for illnesses that more often than not have been caused by poor eating and lack of exercise.

In magazines, we see slim celebrities of all ages looking amazing. The fact is that these photographs have often been doctored or airbrushed to make the celebrities appear slimmer, younger, and normally extra attractive. Don't buy into this. You must never permit yourself to experience inadequacy through measuring yourself against faux media images. They are an illusion. The appearance after yourself through wholesome consumption and exercise will make you avoid a lot of this hype and manipulation.

Clearing Negative Thoughts Technique

CLOSE YOUR EYES and practice your preferred slow deep breathing and relaxation technique, which you should be very familiar with by now. Allow your mind to go blank.

Every time you get an unwanted thought, consider a massive red prevention sign. As soon as you spot the red stop sign, believe the concept is disappearing and your mind becoming clear.

Another thought-clearing technique is to imagine a big computer screen full of data that becomes blank by hitting the delete key. Imagine that by pressing one key you can clear your mind.

You will also find it easier to let go of negative habits because you will only do things congruent with how you feel about yourself. When you feel good about yourself, you will naturally want to cultivate a more positive mindset and have a body that is fit and healthy.

Hypnosis is often described as a control strategy-making people who commit crimes or fall in love. Hypnotists are also generally considered weird magicians. When they hear the word "horse," they put people on stage and let their neighbors. The way hypnosis is expressed in the media may make it appear to be just for entertainment, but hypnosis has more factors than entertainment.

In healthcare, hypnosis can be used as psychotherapy to help you experience changes in feelings, perceptions, thoughts, or behavior. Normally, it includes suggestions for relaxation, calmness, and overall health. Suggestions can last until the meeting, but typical methods can include anything from guiding you to thinking about pleasant experiences or verbal cues to put you in a similar state. Hypnotherapy is a form of therapy that uses hypnosis as a standalone or complementary therapy-can benefit your health in many ways.

Hypnosis can help you solve the following six common health problems:

Trouble Sleeping, Insomnia, and Sleepwalking

If you sleepwalk, have difficulty with falling asleep, and insomnia, hypnosis may be a useful tool. If you have insomnia, it can relax you thoroughly and make it easier for you to fall asleep. If you are a sleepwalker, it can also train you to get up and help you avoid sleepwalking when you feel your foot on the floor.

Moreover, if you want to sleep better, hypnosis can also help you. Learning self-hypnosis techniques can increase your time and deep sleep. It is something that you need to wake up and feel refreshed.

Its working principle is that verbal cues make you in a like state, similar to the feeling that you are addicted to books or movies without feeling what is happening around you. After hypnosis (even during hypnosis), you will fall asleep.

Anxiety

Relaxation techniques—including hypnosis—can sometimes relieve anxiety. Hypnotherapy is often more useful for people whose stress is caused by chronic health conditions (such as heart disease) rather than generalized anxiety. If you suffer from phobias, then hypnotism may also help. Phobia is an anxiety disorder in which you are anxious about things that do not pose a significant threat.

How it works: Hypnosis helps anxiety by encouraging your body to activate its natural relaxation response by using phrases or nonverbal cues, breathing slowly, lowering blood pressure, and instilling overall well-being.

Irritable Bowel Syndrome (IBS) Symptoms

Clinical research has always supported the effectiveness of hypnosis for IBS. It is an abdominal pain caused by the intestine. Hypnosis can help improve symptoms such as constipation, diarrhea, and bloating.

Dr. Grant explained: "IBS can sometimes cause secondary symptoms such as nausea, fatigue, backache, and urinary problems. Hypnotics can also solve these problems."

How it works: Hypnosis will guide you to gradually relax, providing soothing images, and sensations to combat symptoms.

Chronic Pain

Hypnosis can help relieve pain, such as migraine or tension headache after surgery. It can also help relieve chronic pain. People with pain related to diseases such as arthritis, cancer, sickle cell disease, fibromyalgia, and people with lower back problems may be relieved from hypnosis.

How it works: Hypnosis can help you cope with pain and better control your problems. Also, research shows that hypnosis can do this effectively for a long time.

Quit Smoking

Giving up cigarettes is not easy. There are different methods to help you quit smoking, such as nicotine patches or prescription drugs. Although this research is still ongoing, many people find that hypnosis can help them quit smoking. "Grant If you work one-on-one with a hypnotherapist, hypnotherapy can help you quit smoking, and you can customize the hypnosis time according to your lifestyle.

How it works: For hypnotics to quit smoking, you need to quit tobacco honestly. Hypnosis can work in two ways. The first is to help you find healthy and effective alternatives, and then guide your subconscious mind to form the habit instead of smoking. This may be similar to chewing a piece of gum or taking a walk. The second method is to train your mind to associate tobacco with bad feelings, such as a bad taste in your mouth or a foul smell in smoke.

Lose Weight

As with smoking cessation, there are not many studies that confirm the hypnosis effectiveness for weight loss, although some studies have found that hypnosis can reduce a moderate weight—approximately 6 pounds in 18 months. Hypnotherapy is usually most useful when combined with diet and exercise habits.

How it works: After being hypnotized, your attention will be highly concentrated. This makes you more likely to listen to and respond to suggestions about behavior changes, such as eating a healthy diet or doing more exercise, which may help you lose weight.

Tips for Hypnosis Advice

If you make suggestions during self-hypnosis in step 3, follow these tips:

- *Speak firmly:* imagine these words, but be confident, and make sure the tone is reassuring, secure, and positive.

- *The present tense phrase suggestion:* The requirement of "I will be very confident" is more effective than the condition of "I will be very confident" because the word "I" is more specific in the present tense.

- *Make positive suggestions:* For example, "I am at peace" is better than "I have no pressure;" talk to yourself about what you want, not what you don't want.

- *Make practical suggestions:* Avoid making too ambitious suggestions, such as "I will lose a lot of weight quickly." Rather, focus on smaller and more specific goals: "I will eat more vegetables and exercise more."

- *Repeat suggestion:* State the suggestion many times during the hypnosis process. Repeating an idea can help me understand this.

Eat Healthily

Would it be advisable for you to start a better eating routine or create smart dieting propensities to get in shape? For some individuals, the main thing they consider with regards to weight reduction is that they ought to start eating better. In all actuality for long-haul benefits, the propensity for eating nutritiously is a vastly improved alternative for a few reasons.

The very notice of "starting a better eating routine" infers that you will later fall off of that diet. That in that spot reveals to you that eating fewer carbs is a momentary way to deal with a way of life issue. Sure, craze diets may work for the time being, yet over the long haul, they, for the most part, don't give any genuine advantage. Individuals need to shed pounds and keep it off. By learning the best possible strategies for weight control and keeping up smart dieting propensities, you are substantially more liable to reach and remain at your ideal weight. Giving exceptionally nutritious foods in the best possible sums is the ideal approach to fuel your body and control your weight.

Many "prevailing fashion eats less" increase momentary fame for the straightforward explanation that they give present moment, quick weight reduction, these eating regimens are frequently founded on taking out some nutritious foods and supplanting them with shakes, caffeinated drinks or other enchantment elixirs, diet pills, high fiber blends or costly prepared dinners. Some of the time, definitely diminishing your calories is a piece of these weight control plans. It is imperative to recollect that your body is powered by the nourishment you eat. To work at an elevated level, be solid and enthusiastic, it is indispensable to supply your body with exceptionally nutritious foods. Expelling nutritious foods from your eating regimen in a hurry to get more fit can't insightful choice. At times quick weight reduction can accomplish more mischief than anything.

A great many people comprehend that your body's digestion is imperative to weight control. Think about your digestion as your degree of vitality use. Utilizing less energy can prompt weight gain since the muscle to fat ratio is an abundance of vitality that gets put away in fat cells. By diminishing weight too quickly it can make your body hinder your digestion.

This, thus, can make you sleep weight after the underlying quick weight reduction of an eating routine. Known as the yo-yo impact, this is a main source of disappointment for people hoping to get thinner and keep it off. By joining appropriate dietary patterns and reasonable exercise, you can successfully keep up your digestion working at its legitimate level, which will help with controlling your weight. Muscle-fortifying activity, which straightforwardly expands your digestion, is significant, as is normal cardio aerobic exercise.

A couple of key focuses on appropriate eating ought to be remembered. Eating a few generally little estimated dinners and snacks for the day is a superior methodology than bigger, less continuous suppers. Try not to skip breakfast - it truly is the most significant dinner of the day. Eating normally keeps up your digestion. Select crisp foods and genuine items, including natural food sources, are vastly improved nourishment decisions than exceptionally handled, substance, and sodium-filled foods.

Numerous individuals believe that eating nutritiously is hard to achieve. The methodology one should take is to create good dieting propensities to get in shape, keep up legitimate weight, and augment your wellbeing. Propensities, both great and awful, are difficult to break. When you set up great dietary patterns, those propensities will be generally simple to keep up for the basic season; your eating techniques are only that - a propensity. Some portion of building up a decent nourishing project is figuring out how to basic food items look for good nourishment decisions. Most visits to the market lead you to similar paths and choosing similar nourishment things. By becoming accustomed to continually purchasing a choice of sound, nutritious foods, it will guarantee that you have these things in your home.

Another misinterpretation about appropriate eating is that nutritious foods are exhausting, tasteless, and not delicious. Nothing can be further from reality. Legitimate nourishment arrangements, cooking techniques, nutritious plans, and sound nourishment substitution can prompt some amazingly solid and delectable dishes.

With the best possible disposition towards your wholesome propensities, it very well may be an enjoyment, sound, and delicious approach to legitimate weight control. The feared "starting a better eating routine" approach can stay away from as you create smart dieting designs on your approach to great wellbeing and legitimate weight reduction.

If you record what you are regularly eating, you presumably will drop your jaw with sickening apprehension. We never think to include the little tad portion size piece of candy here and the two treats to observe the significant effect it is having on our weight control plans. The ideal approach to accomplish a solid way of life, to the extent our weight control plans go, is eating more products of the soil. We as a whole know it, so for what reason do we head for the potato chips aisle in the supermarket rather than the produce segment?

Essentially it comes down to this. Low-quality foods trigger our craving and leave us aching for additional. Ever wonder why eating one minimal honest Cheez-it prompts eating a large portion of a case? One taste triggers your body to need to continue eating. Presently if you could condition yourself to do that with red grapes, we could accomplish that solid way of life. It might be hard to do, however, not feasible. Here are five different ways to condition yourself to settle on more beneficial nibble decisions.

Out Of Sight, Out Of Mind

If you don't have good nourishment in your kitchen, you won't eat it. It truly is that straightforward. I am the sort of individual who needs something to eat while I watch my daily film, and I will, in general, get the terrible stuff. The main occasions I don't is the point at which I cannot. Do your shopping for food directly after you have eaten an enormous supper so you won't be eager for awful foods, yet rather great food sources. Leave the store with no low-quality nourishment yet with plenty of products fresh. Your handbag and your tummy will thank you over the long haul.

Add Fruits And Vegetables To Your Dishes

Some of the time, it is difficult to plunk down with a couple of strawberries without the chocolate plunge; you desire something terrible. That is the trigger nourishment shouting to you; however, you need not answer. Cut the strawberries up and add them to a bowl of oat. Toss in a couple of blueberries and raisins. Simply make sure to utilize skim milk and keep the sugar in the cabinet. Organic product has enough normal sweetness without anyone else. Consider it characteristic treats.

When was the last time you are excited to eat carrot and celery sticks without plunging sauce? Likely never, yet that doesn't mean you never will. Add them to a little serving of mixed greens when you need a tad portion. No, you cannot suffocate it all in greasy blue cheddar dressing.

That is a similar thing as plunge, is it not? A tad of vinaigrette dressing is the thing that your psyche ought to consider.

Make a Compromise

If you are following the American Diet, your palette presently pines for high salt and high sugar foods. Stopping is never fruitful when it is done immediately. Individuals think they have to stop all the awful stuff at the same time and afterward three days after the fact they wear out and return to negative behavior patterns. Being sound can't pass up the foods you love.

On the off chance that you need pizza, eat a cat with a bowl of natural product serving of mixed greens rather than French fries. If you need Cheeze-Its, eat a bunch with a bunch of grapes rather than a large portion of the cheez-It box. Straightforwardness into it and gradually improve your dietary patterns.

Load up on Liquids

Commonly we mistake strive after thirst. You think you are hungry until you drink a decent, reviving glass of water. At that point, your stomach feels somewhat fuller, and you have not included more calories in your midsection line. On the off chance that you make sure to drink fluids regularly, you will likely get yourself not in any event, thinking you are eager any longer.

So in light of that, whenever you fear to request an excess of fettuccine Alfredo at your preferred Italian eatery, drink a tall glass of water before you request. You may want to pass that for a pleasant fresh plate of mixed greens with shrimp or chicken.

Take A Supplement

Once in a while, we get going in our lives and may have the best expectations to eat healthily; however, we cannot generally find solid foods to eat. Most candy machines don't offer carrot and celery sticks, shockingly. One route around this is to take a day by day supplement that gives all of you the sustenance you would get on the off chance that you ate heaps of products of the soil. This doesn't mean you should take them and keep eating giggles bars throughout the day, as you may have guessed. Garbage is still garbage.

Eating foods grown from the ground may not be something you are utilized to, however simply like whatever else, it takes some becoming accustomed to. Utilize the tips above to make progress simpler, yet don't take on a similar mindset as a con artist. Con artists never succeed, and if it was simple, everybody would stroll around in very good shape. Carrying on with a sound way of life implies settling on solid decisions. The more you can do it, the more benefits you will be.

Chapter 12. Frequently Asked Questions

Can I Use Hypnosis To Lose Weight?

Weight loss hypnosis can help you lose excess weight if it is part of a weight-loss plan that includes diet, exercise, and counseling. Hypnosis is usually done with the help of a hypnotherapist using repeated words and spiritual images.

How Well Does Hypnosis Work For Weight Loss?

For those who want to lose weight, hypnosis may be more effective than just eating and exercising. The idea is that it can affect the mind to change habits like overeating. The researchers concluded that hypnosis may promote weight loss, but there is not enough research to convince it.

Is Hypnosis Dangerous?

Hypnosis performed by a trained therapist or medical professional is considered a safe and complementary alternative. However, hypnosis may not be appropriate for people with severe mental illness. The side effects of hypnosis are rare, but may include the following:

Can Hypnosis Change Your Personality?

No, hypnosis doesn't work at all. But that is a fun premise. That said, hypnosis helps with stress, bad (and good) habits, sleep deprivation and quality, and pain management. In that case, no, hypnosis cannot change personality.

How Can I Tell If Someone Is Hypnotized?

The following changes do not always occur in all hypnotic subjects, but most are seen sometime during the trance experience.

- Stare.

- Pupil dilation.

- Change in blinking reflection.

- Rapid eye movement.

- The eyelids flutter.

- Smoothing facial muscles.

- Breathing slows down.

- Reduced swallowing reflex.

How Long Does It Take For Hypnosis To Work?

Depending on what the client's goal is, the client will appear on average between 4-12 sessions. Imagine for some time that you are my client and that you are sitting in my comfortable "hypnotic chair".

What Are The Negative Effects Of Hypnosis?

There are several risks associated with hypnosis. The most dangerous is the possibility of creating incorrect memories (called confabulations). Other potential side effects include headache, dizziness, and anxiety. But these usually disappear immediately after the hypnosis session

What Is The Hypnosis Success Rate?

The study found that hypnosis had long-term changes in an average of six hypnosis sessions, while psychoanalysis took 600 times. Also, hypnosis was very effective. After 6 sessions, 93% of participants had a recovery rate of only 38% in the psychoanalysis group.

Does Hypnosis Work When I Sleep?

Hypnosis does not sleep (a meditation with a goal), but if you are tired, you can fall asleep while listening to hypnosis. Fortunately, hypnosis reaches the subconscious even if it falls asleep

How Much Weight Can I Lose With Hypnosis?

Most studies show a slight weight loss, with an average loss of about 6 pounds (2.7 kilograms) over 18 months. However, the quality of some of these studies has been questioned and it is difficult to determine the true effectiveness of weight loss hypnosis.

Does Meditation Lose Weight?

Although there isn't a lot of research that shows that meditation can directly help you lose weight, meditation can help you better understand your thoughts and actions, including those related to food.

For example, research reviews have shown that meditation can help with both bulimia and an emotional diet

Can Everyone Be Hypnotized?

If we understand hypnosis as a focused state of attention, where there is not necessarily a loss of consciousness or lack of memory about what has happened in the session, the answer is yes. But if we understand this question as if the whole world can reach deep trance (sleepwalking) - understood in terms of classical hypnosis - with practically total suggestibility and loss of consciousness, the answer would be a relative NO.

Getting a light or medium trance is relatively easy. Reaching a deep trance is more complex; approximately 80% of subjects can reach a deep stage without much difficulty. The remaining 20% would be difficult due to several complicated variables of knowing or controlling (fear of losing one's conscience, prejudices or beliefs, lack of confidence in the inducer, etc.) Despite this fact, if we use hypnosis at the clinical level or doctor, in most cases a medium trance is enough to obtain results 2.- Who can hypnotize?

Hypnosis is essentially a technique. Therefore, anyone who knows it enough and learns to apply it can hypnotize. Another thing is that the inductor can then confront and solve the different situations that arise during the session. If the hypnotist does not have concrete and sufficient theoretical-practical knowledge (even if they are doctors or psychologists), it could cause serious damage to the hypnotist. Even more so if the inducer pursues unlawful ends and tries to violate the physical, psychic, or moral integrity of the inducer, which has happened numerous times, manipulating the hypnotized.

In some countries, clinical hypnosis is only allowed to doctors and psychologists previously authorized and prepared.

Can Someone Fall Asleep Forever?

It can't happen. Whether we practice self-hypnosis (about ourselves), or hetero-hypnosis, that is, about another person, we will always end up leaving the hypnotic state. If for any reason the hypnotist disappeared, the induced subject would progressively move from the hypnotic trance to natural sleep and would gradually wake up and clear. It happens sometimes that the person is in such a placid situation that he resists waking up. In that case, we can make a counter-suggestion such as: "If you want to stay or return to this state in the future, you must wake up now" - and will normally abandon hypnosis. Or we just let it rest until it wakes up after a time that is usually short.

Does Hypnosis Have Contraindications?

Hypnosis and all similar states and techniques produce a great benefit to the organism since it helps eliminate physical or emotional tensions, slightly reduces blood pressure, regulates the heart and respiratory rhythm, balances the cerebral hemispheres and if we talk in energetic terms, rebalances the body's bioenergy. Therefore, if we are normally healthy people, we will not be in any danger.

However, there are two absolute indications: in general, hypnosis should not be performed on people with schizophrenia or serious mental illness. Why? Because we could aggravate their symptoms apart from that they would be difficult to induce.

The second case is about people with epilepsy or who have had recent crises of this type: during hypnosis one of these crises could occur, so prudence advises not to submit them.
5.- Does the hypnotist have any special power?

Strongly NO. When hypnosis is used as a show, the hypnotist usually presents himself with an aura of exceptional mental powers; This is part of the suggestive environment that the inductor will use to achieve its spectacular effects. It all depends on how suggestible and impressionable we are.

If a person does not want it, it is very difficult to be induced, unless there is such an extreme fear or conviction that the hypnotist has such (fictitious) power that our own belief or conviction will make us fall into hypnosis even sometimes instantaneously to the slightest suggestion or touch of the inductor. To hypnotize you do not need special skills, but a minimum of skills. For example, a shy, doubtful, and insecure person would be a bad hypnotist or hypnotist.

Can Someone Be Induced To Do What They Do Not Want?

Although several authors deny this possibility, our practice only for experimental purposes shows us that YES. Everything depends on many different variables, but if the induced subject has a sufficient degree of hypnotic depth, he can accept, in whole or in part, the possibility of refusing the suggestions imposed by the hypnotist. There have been numerous cases of rape and mental manipulation under states of hypnosis - this is nothing new - That is why we should not be hypnotized by people who do not have our confidence.

Can We Hypnotize Ourselves?

Of course. Self-hypnosis is one of the most interesting aspects of this technique. For this we can use - for example - a cassette, where we will record an induction to relax progressively, including suggestions such as: "I am getting calmer, my muscles are released, little by little I feel a pleasant and deep reverie. "In the end, we will add the suggestions that we want to implement for various purposes, such as studying more and better, quitting tobacco, being calmer, etc.

Can You Hypnotize Us Without Us Noticing?

Hypnosis is more present in our lives than we imagine. If this is only a state of attention more or less acute and focused, every day we suffer to a greater or lesser extent one or more "hypnosis." Advertising - especially on TV aims to hypnotize us (suggest us) to buy a product. Politicians use very elaborate communication and image techniques to capture our attention, even where the final impression is more important than the speech itself. But returning to classical hypnosis, there are subliminal techniques to induce a subject to hypnotic states and induce him, without the need for loss of consciousness - to certain behavior or attitude.

Is There Instant Hypnosis?

Yes. For example, in hypnotic shows, when the inductor realizes that someone among his audience is very suggestible and even shows some fear when approaching him, his fear and the fact that the hypnotist is seen wearing a special power, will make the slightest hint of it, the viewer immediately falls into hypnosis (normally it will be a light or medium trance and will have to be deepened).

The other case would be when once induction is achieved, the subject is left implanted with a post-hypnotic order such as: "when you wake up and on the next occasions when I tell you, you will immediately fall into this same state" If the achieved state is deep enough, it is implanted in the subject's deep mind and can last even for an indefinite period.

Can You Hypnotize from A Distance?

This is one of the most fascinating research fields in the field. It is disturbing to see that on many occasions under hypnosis mental activity, its scope and scope of knowledge will exceed space and time. Our nervous system is a true network through which low voltage electricity circulates; where there is electricity, electro-magnetism can be given, so that the network of extended neurons throughout our anatomy becomes a virtual frequency transmitter that can incorporate certain information.

Conclusion

Hypnosis for weight loss is some things that you simply got to have in your life. It'll allow you to vary your dieting and eating habits, and by the top of it, you'll even be ready to have a far better time when it involves your control of food.

Remember, this isn't only for your benefit when it involves the amount that's seen on the size, but it'll also benefit you by having the ability to vary your outlook on life.

You don't get to think that the sole thing to do is to only persist with the diet you're on. Couple it with hypnosis for weight loss, and you'll have a good better time. It'll make all the more difference in your life also.

Hypnosis for weight loss is the best way to reduce it. You'll be ready to break down, and you'll even be prepared to take hold of your eating habits. Remember, this also reduces stress, and you'll control the way you think that about things too. It's how to vary the general outlook of life, and it's also an excellent way to allow yourself the power to have the ability to possess a far better experience that's crammed with happiness. You'll lose that weight, and it starts together with your ability to figure on your hypnosis for weight loss regimen.

The next step is to start out performing on your weight and diet. You ought to ask a doctor before doing this, simply because it's a sensible thing to do, but once you're through with that, you'll start performing on it. You should also confirm that you simply have a healthy diet plan and an exercise plan already in situ because which will allow you to possess a far better time with this. once you have all three of these, the pounds will drop feel happier.

It's time to require control of your life, and with this, you'll be ready to change your eating habits for the higher. Hypnosis for weight loss is straightforward to do, but if you're unsure of doing it on your own, you'll see a counselor about it. But, it's a way that's so simple, you don't need plenty of direction to do it.

CPSIA information can be obtained
at www.ICGtesting.com
Printed in the USA
BVHW060910250321
603396BV00008B/583

9 781801 850667